Victorian Memories

In Cross Stitch & Needlepoint

Victorian Memories

In Cross Stitch & Needlepoint

Chris Timms

CLB

Colour Library Books

To my parents

CLB 4311

This edition published in 1994 for
Colour Library Books Ltd
Godalming Business Centre
Woolsack Way
Godalming
Surrey GU7 1XW

ISBN 1 85833 234 6

Conceived, edited and designed by Collins & Brown Limited

Editor: *Eleanor Van Zandt*

Designed by: *Peter Bridgewater*

Filmset by Servis Filmsetting Ltd, Manchester
Reproduction by Scantrans, Singapore
Printed and bound in Italy by New Interlitho SpA

Contents

Foreword

The nostalgia evoked by Chris Timms's subtle designs has its roots in the way she lives, at the heart of a large and beautiful family, whose exuberant activities echo her own childhood. Always in tune with the intricacies of changing style, she opens up her knowledge to the readers of this delightful book so that they may creatively enjoy the pleasures it depicts.

LYN LE GRICE
Penzance, 1993

Introduction

Cross stitch and needlepoint, or tapestry, are relaxing and simple forms of embroidery. If you can count, and pull a needle and thread in and out of a hole, you can make any project in this book! My favourite subjects are children, the sea and farm animals, and

Crab Pincushion

these are all reflected in my designs. I have lived in the country for most of my adult life, and although my family and I now live in a town, we are on the sea front, and I can see boats from my windows. So if you live in a city and yearn for the countryside or the sea, you can bring images of them into your house with these designs. They will be a reminder of holidays gone by and an antidote to the traffic and tower blocks.

I have tried in this book to provide projects to appeal both to those who have never attempted this kind of work and to those who already enjoy it. They include some larger projects – to attract the more experienced needleworker – and small projects, such as bookmarks and paperweights, that are not too daunting and can be quickly and easily stitched and made up into useful objects to keep yourself or to give as presents. This will, I hope, encourage beginners to progress to the more

Farmyard Sampler

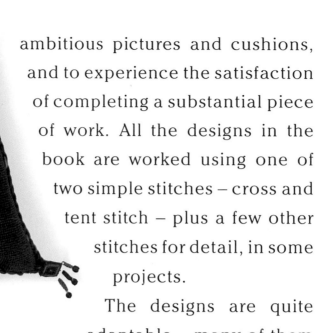

Flowers in Tall Vase Cushion

ambitious pictures and cushions, and to experience the satisfaction of completing a substantial piece of work. All the designs in the book are worked using one of two simple stitches – cross and tent stitch – plus a few other stitches for detail, in some projects.

The designs are quite adaptable – many of them may be worked either on evenweave fabric or on needlepoint canvas, depending on individual choice. Some are designed to be worked small scale, on fine fabric or canvas, and will suit those with good eyesight who like to embroider tiny, intricate designs; others use coarser fabric and will be preferred by those who find small stitches hard on the eyes.

Many of the designs can be adapted in various ways. For example, some of the simpler borders and motifs could be worked on Aida band – or on any chosen evenweave material – and made up into a bookmark or a set of napkin rings, or applied to the bodice of a child's dress or the edge of a sheet or pillowcase. They could also be used for such items as jam pot covers, herb sachets or table napkins.

I hope that you will enjoy making and adapting these projects as much as I enjoyed designing them.

*Rocking Horse and Girl
with Snowball Tree Decorations*

SEASIDE
Memories

WHEN I WAS A CHILD, *I could not sleep for excitement the night before we went on holiday to the seaside. And the excitement grew to fever pitch as we neared Llanelli, in South Wales, where my aunt and uncle lived.*
We spent many happy days on the unspoilt beaches of the nearby Gower Peninsula – glorious days picnicking at Port-Eynon, leaping in the surf at Llangennith and walking the long, windswept sands of Rhossili, where sea pinks grew on the cliffs.
I used to enjoy digging for mussels and cockles with my uncle. You could tell where the cockles were by the dozens of tiny holes in the sand.

Boys on the Beach Greetings Card

This greetings card will evoke happy memories for anyone who has ever enjoyed playing on a sandy beach – and who hasn't?

MATERIALS
DMC stranded embroidery cotton, one skein each of the following colours:

794	sky blue
793	mid-blue
3364	light green
3790	brown
948	flesh pink
950	dark flesh pink
797	dark blue
554	lilac
315	maroon
3047	pale yellow
3046	yellow
924	dark green
blanc neige	white

- Piece of 16-count white Aida cloth, 18×12cm (7×5in)
- Tapestry needle, size 24
- Greetings card for embroidery, 16×11cm ($6\frac{1}{4} \times 4\frac{3}{8}$in), with rectangular opening 11×7cm ($4\frac{3}{8} \times 2\frac{3}{4}$in)
- White glue stick

SIZE
The design measures 11×7cm ($4\frac{3}{8} \times 2\frac{3}{4}$in).

TO MAKE THE CARD
Work the design in cross stitch, following the chart and using two strands of thread. Each square represents one stitch.

Press the completed work. Insert it in the card following the instructions on page 124.

	924	dark green
	3364	light green
	797	dark blue
	793	mid-blue
	794	sky blue
	554	lilac
	315	maroon
	950	dark flesh pink
	948	flesh pink
	3047	pale yellow
	3046	yellow
	3790	brown
	blanc neige	white

Crab Pincushion

The crab design on this pincushion is worked in Assisi embroidery, a traditional method in which the motif is left blank and the background filled in with cross stitch.

SIZE
The pincushion measures about 8 × 8cm (3 × 3in).

TO MAKE THE PINCUSHION
Fold the material in half across its width so that it measures 9 × 10.5cm (3½ × 4in). Work the design on one half, beginning with the Holbein stitch outline (see page 117) and positioning the top line six fabric threads from the fold. Fill in with cross stitch. You can use either two or three strands of thread. Each square of the chart represents one stitch worked over *three* threads of the fabric.

Press the completed work, and make up the pincushion following the instructions on page 121.

VARIATION
The crab motif could be worked in cross stitch, at a larger scale, against a plain background, in realistic colours, and used, for example, on the pocket of an apron.

MATERIALS
DMC stranded embroidery cotton, one skein of the following colour:

924 *green*

- Piece of 28-count *eau-de-nil* evenweave cloth, 18 × 10.5cm (7 × 4in)
- Tapestry needle, size 26
- Piece of 2.5cm (1in)-thick wadding, 18 × 10.5cm (7 × 4in), plus another piece, 9 × 10.5cm (3½ × 4in)
- Small amount of pot-pourri

924 green   + = centre of design

Sail Bookmark

This bookmark would make a good present for anyone who sails – or just dreams of sailing.

MATERIALS

DMC stranded embroidery cotton, one skein each of the following colours:

519	*sky blue*
739	*cream*
3761	*pale sea blue*
793	*dark sea blue*
452	*grey*
561	*green*
819	*pink*
blanc neige	*white*

- Piece of 15-count, 5cm (2in)-wide cream Aida band, 23cm (9in) long
- Tapestry needle, size 24
- Piece of thin lining fabric, 17.5 × 6cm (7 × 2¼in)

SIZE

The design measures 16.5cm (6½in) long.

TO MAKE THE BOOKMARK

Work the design in cross stitch, following the chart and using two strands of thread. Each square represents one stitch.

Press the completed work. Apply the lining and finish the ends of the Aida band following the instructions on page 121.

A wet sheet and a flowing sea,
A wind that blows fast,
And fills the white and rustling sail,
And bends the gallant mast.

At Sea, ALLAN CUNNINGHAM

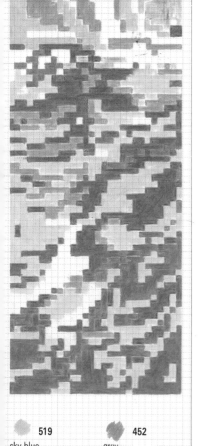

519 sky blue	452 grey
3761 pale sea blue	819 pink
793 dark sea blue	739 cream
561 green	blanc neige white

Seabird Sampler

Terns, shelduck, sea pinks, sea lavender and a velvet swimming crab, surrounded by a border of golden samphire, make a sampler that evokes life along the seashore.

415	*light grey*
414	*mid-grey*
413	*dark grey*
726	*yellow*
972	*orange*
632	*brown*
938	*dark brown*
334	*bright blue*
931	*smoke blue*
926	*turquoise green*
223	*pink*
5200	*white*

- Piece of 28-count cream evenweave cloth, 36 × 30cm (14 × 12in)
- Tapestry needle, size 26
- Piece of card, 30 × 23cm (12 × 9in)
- Strong thread

SIZE
The sampler measures 30 × 23cm (12 × 9in).

TO MAKE THE SAMPLER
Work the design in cross stitch, following the chart and using two strands of thread. Each square represents one stitch, worked over two fabric threads.

Press the completed work. Mount it over the card (see page 121) and place it in a frame.

MATERIALS
DMC stranded embroidery cotton, one skein each of the following colours:

471	*light green*
3347	*apple green*

413 dark grey		926 turquoise green		3347 apple green		972 orange		938 dark brown
414 mid-grey		334 bright blue		471 light green		223 pink		5200 white
415 light grey		931 smoke blue		726 yellow		632 brown		+ = centre of design

Boy and Dog Picture

Playing on the seashore with the waves lapping at your feet is even more fun if you've got a four-legged friend to play with.

MATERIALS
DMC stranded embroidery cotton in the following colours:

blanc neige	white
341	blue
793	dark blue
841	light brown
948	light flesh pink
950	dark flesh pink
3045	yellow ochre
3790	dark brown
3052	light green
3051	dark green
413	dark grey
(one skein each)	
3753	sky blue
3752	sea blue
(two skeins each)	

● Piece of 14-count white Aida cloth, 38 × 31cm (15 × 12in)
● Tapestry needle, size 24
● Piece of card, 23 × 16cm (9 × 6¼in)
● Strong thread

SIZE
The picture measures 23 × 16cm (9 × 6¼in).

413 dark grey

793 dark blue

341 blue

3752 sea blue

3753 sky blue

blanc neige white

948 light flesh pink

950 dark flesh pink

3045 yellow ochre

841 light brown

3790 dark brown

3052 light green

3051 dark green

For every wave upon the sands
Sings songs you never tire to hear,
Of laden ships from sunny lands
Where it is summer all the year.

The World's Music,
GABRIEL SETOUN

TO MAKE THE PICTURE
Work the design in cross
stitch, following the chart
and using two strands of
thread. Each square
represents one stitch.
 Press the completed work,
mount it over the card (see
page 121) and place it in a
frame.

VARIATION
This design could also be
worked in tent stitch, using
tapestry wool on canvas.
(See the stranded cotton–
tapestry wool colour
conversion chart on
page 127.)

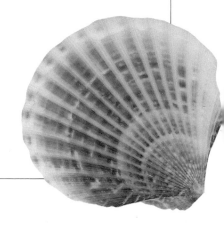

Sand Castle Picture

Everyone can help to build a sand castle – or so Fido seems to think! This lively scene will recall happy summer days all year round.

MATERIALS

DMC stranded embroidery cotton in the following colours:

793	*sea blue*
312	*dark blue*
blanc neige	*white*
948	*light flesh pink*
950	*dark flesh pink*
3743	*lilac*
3041	*dark lilac*
413	*dark grey*
414	*light grey*
841	*brown*
502	*green*
3713	*pink*
(one skein each)	
3752	*sky blue*
3047	*light sand*
3046	*dark sand*
(two skeins each)	

- Piece of 14-count white Aida cloth, 30 × 30cm (12 × 12in)
- Tapestry needle, size 24
- Piece of card, 22 × 22cm (8½ × 8½in)
- Strong thread

SIZE

The picture measures 22 × 22cm (8½ × 8½in).

TO MAKE THE PICTURE

Work the design in cross stitch, following the chart and using two strands of thread. Each square represents one stitch.

Press the completed work, mount it over card (see page 121) and place it in a frame.

VARIATION

This design could also be worked in tent stitch, using tapestry wool on canvas. (See the colour conversion chart on page 127.)

*B*uild me a castle of sand
Down by the sea.
Here on the edge of the strand
Build it for me.

Sand Castles, W. GRAHAM ROBERTSON

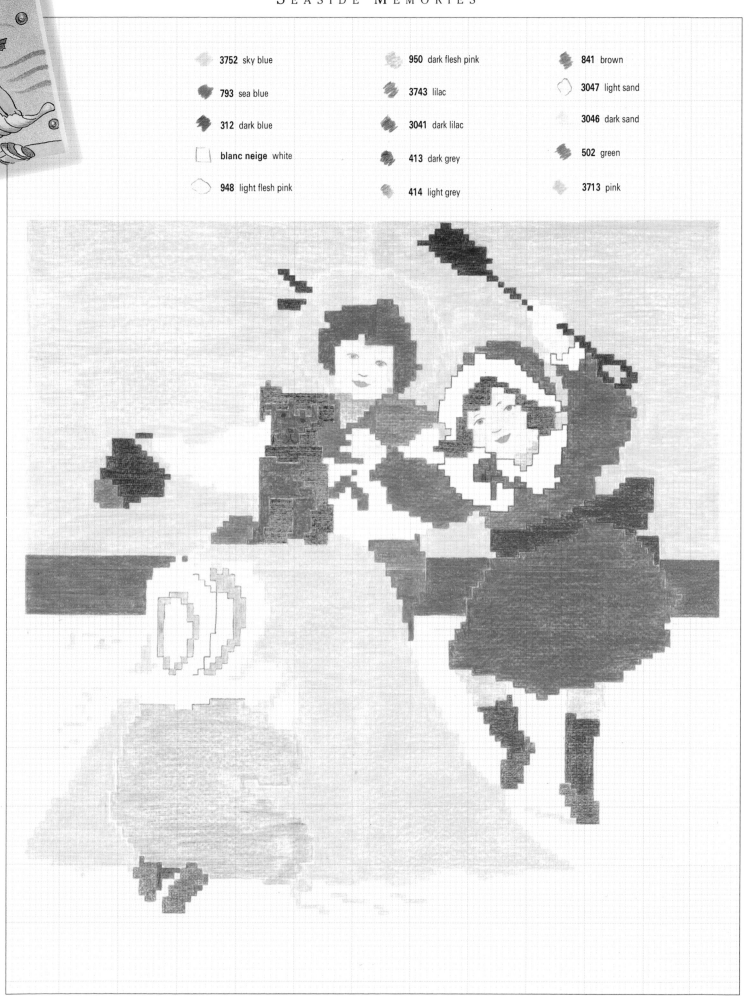

3752 sky blue		**950** dark flesh pink		**841** brown	
793 sea blue		**3743** lilac		**3047** light sand	
312 dark blue		**3041** dark lilac		**3046** dark sand	
blanc neige white		**413** dark grey		**502** green	
948 light flesh pink		**414** light grey		**3713** pink	

CHART ON PAGES 24–5

Sailing Picture

Ocean breezes fill the sail of the little craft in this
needlepoint picture. It is worked in tent stitch, using
stranded cotton.

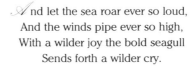

And let the sea roar ever so loud,
And the winds pipe ever so high,
With a wilder joy the bold seagull
Sends forth a wilder cry.

The Seagull, MARY HOWITT

CHART ON PAGES 26–7

Sailor Boy Picture

All the excitement of going to sea in the old days, on a tall ship, is evoked in this picture of a sailor and a young lad. It is worked on fine canvas using tent stitch.

*O*h, the wind is wild and the waves are high,
And it's time for the sailor boy to say 'Goodbye!'
With a kiss for his Mother, and the rest at home,
Then away and away on the rolling foam.
Ah, the world may be happy, but its brightest joy
Is found in the heart of a sailor boy.

ANON

CHART FOR SAILING PICTURE

MATERIALS
DMC stranded embroidery cotton in the following colours:

3781	*dark brown*
930	*indigo blue*
931	*Prussian blue*
543	*flesh pink*
840	*bronze*
3047	*yellow*
926	*deep sea green*
écru	*cream*
(one skein each)	
407	*dark rust*
3772	*red*
793	*dark sea blue*
794	*sea blue*
927	*light sea green*
(two skeins each)	
blanc neige	*white*
(three skeins)	
3773	*rust*
3753	*sky blue*
(five skeins each)	

● Piece of 18-gauge white single-thread or interlock canvas, 38 × 38cm (15 × 15in)
● Tapestry needle, size 26
● Piece of card, 25 × 25cm (10 × 10in)
● Strong thread

SIZE
The picture measures 25 × 25cm (10 × 10in).

TO MAKE THE PICTURE
Work the design in tent stitch, following the chart and using all six strands of thread. Each square represents one stitch.

Block the completed work (see page 120). Mount it over the card (see page 121) and place it in a frame.

3753 sky blue

794 sea blue

793 dark sea blue

931 Prussian blue

930 indigo blue

927 light sea green

926 deep sea green

écru cream

543 flesh pink

3047 yellow

3773 rust

407 dark rust

840 bronze

3781 dark brown

3772 red

blanc neige white

648 dark grey

762 light grey

452 pink-brown

blanc neige white

415 mid-grey

453 light pink-brown

948 pale flesh pink

3774 mid-flesh pink

950 dark flesh pink

224 pink

739 ochre

3047 light yellow

3046 deep yellow

341 blue

793 dark sea blue

794 light sea blue

930 dark blue

502 green

841 brown

840 dark brown

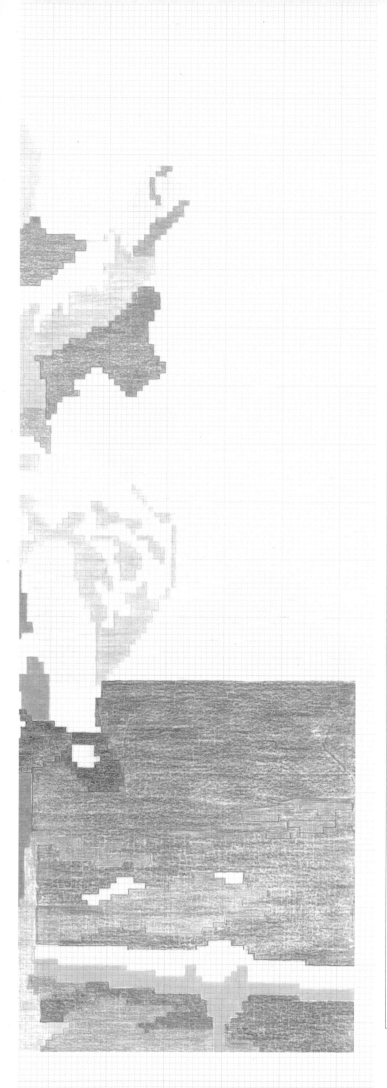

CHART
FOR SAILOR BOY PICTURE

MATERIALS
DMC stranded embroidery cotton in the following colours:

840	dark brown
841	brown
3047	light yellow
3046	deep yellow
930	dark blue
648	dark grey
794	light sea blue
948	pale flesh pink
950	deep flesh pink
3774	mid-flesh pink
224	pink
452	pink-brown
453	light pink-brown
415	mid-grey
502	green
(one skein each)	
341	blue
762	light grey
739	ochre
(two skeins each)	
793	dark sea blue
(three skeins)	
blanc neige white	
(eight skeins)	

● Piece of 18-gauge white single-thread or interlock canvas, 43 × 40cm (17 × 16in)
● Tapestry needle, size 26
● Piece of card, 26 × 24cm (10¼ × 9½in)
● Strong thread

SIZE
The picture measures 26 × 24cm (10¼ × 9½in).

TO MAKE THE PICTURE
Work the design in tent stitch, following the chart and using all six strands of the stranded cotton. Each square represents one stitch.

Block the work (see page 120). Mount the picture over the card (see page 121), and place it in a frame.

VARIATIONS
The design could be worked in cross stitch on evenweave cloth, using two or three strands of thread, depending on the count of the chosen cloth. It could also be worked in tapestry wool, using tent stitch on 10- or 12-gauge canvas. It will be much larger; for example, 10-gauge canvas will make a picture 46 × 43cm (18 × 17in). (See the stranded cotton–tapestry wool colour conversion chart on page 127.)

CHART ON PAGES 30–1

Shrimping Picture

On a bright summer day, with a gentle breeze
whipping up whitecaps, it's fun to go shrimping, then
bring your catch home for lunch.

The sun was shining on the sea,
 Shining with all his might:
 He did his very best to make
 The billows smooth and bright –

The sea was wet as wet could be,
 The sands were dry as dry.
You could not see a cloud, because
 No cloud was in the sky.

The Walrus and the Carpenter, LEWIS CARROLL

CHART ON PAGES 32-3

Canoeing Cushion

This cushion design captures the excitement of
racing canoes through choppy water.

7404 green

7301 sky blue

7593 grey-blue

7285 pale grey

7813 blue

7543 flesh pink

7745	yellow		7162	light brown		7758	pink
7492	light sand		7232	mid-brown		7266	purple
7523	dark sand		7432	brown		blanc	white

CHART FOR SHRIMPING PICTURE

MATERIALS
DMC tapestry wool (Laine Colbert) in the following colours:

7523	*dark sand*
blanc	*white*
7285	*pale grey*
7266	*purple*
7162	*light brown*
7432	*brown*
7593	*grey-blue*
7543	*flesh pink*
7404	*green*
7758	*pink*
7745	*yellow*
(one skein each)	
7232	*mid-brown*
(two skeins)	
7492	*light sand*
7301	*sky blue*
(three skeins each)	
7813	*blue*
(four skeins)	

● Piece of 10-gauge white single-thread or interlock canvas, 40 × 50cm (16 × 20in)
● Tapestry needle, size 22
● Piece of card, 24 × 35cm ($9\frac{1}{2}$ × 14in)
● Strong thread

SIZE
The picture measures 24 × 35cm ($9\frac{1}{2}$ × 14in).

TO MAKE THE PICTURE
Work the design in tent stitch, following the chart and using one strand of thread. Each square represents one stitch.

Block the work (see page 120), mount it over the card (see page 121) and place it in a frame.

CHART FOR CANOEING CUSHION

MATERIALS

DMC tapestry wool (Laine Colbert) in the following colours:

7511	*blonde*
7413	*dark blonde*
7416	*dark brown*
7162	*light flesh pink*
7463	*deep flesh pink*
7504	*light yellow*
7473	*dark yellow*
blanc	*white*
(one skein each)	
7402	*light green*
7184	*dark red*
7692	*mid-blue*
7392	*mid-green*
(two skeins each)	
7301	*light blue*
7306	*dark blue*
7920	*light red*
(three skeins each)	
7396	*dark green*
(four skeins)	

● Piece of 10-gauge single-thread or interlock canvas, 56 × 56cm (22 × 22in)
● Tapestry needle, size 22
● Piece of velvet, or other furnishing fabric, 48 × 48cm (19 × 19in)
● Four strips of the same fabric, each 48 × 8.5cm (19 × 3¼in)
● 2m (2¼yd) of 1cm (⅜in)-diameter furnishing braid
● Cushion pad 45 × 45cm (18 × 18in)

SIZE

The design measures 35 × 35cm (14 × 14in). The cushion measures 44 × 44cm (17½ × 17½in).

⬉   ⬈

TO MAKE THE CUSHION
Work the design in tent
stitch, following the chart
and using a single strand
of thread. Each square
represents one stitch.
   Block the completed work
(see page 120). Make up the
cushion following the
instructions on page 122.

VARIATION
This design would be equally
successful as a picture,
worked either in tapestry
wool or in stranded cotton
on evenweave. (See the
stranded cotton–tapestry
wool colour conversion chart
on page 127.)

⬋   ⬊

7396 dark green

7392 mid-green

7402 light green

7301 light blue

7692 mid-blue

7306 dark blue

7184 dark red

7920 light red

7473 dark yellow

7504 light yellow

7162 light flesh pink

7463 deep flesh pink

7511 blonde

7413 dark blonde

7416 dark brown

blanc white

CHART ON PAGES 36–7

Beach Tents Picture

This picture has a lot of detail and uses thirty-one colours, but I think its sense of activity makes it fun to ·stitch.

MATERIALS

DMC tapestry wool (Laine Colbert) in the following colours:

7226	*maroon*
7266	*dark maroon*
7451	*pale flesh pink*
7590	*deep flesh pink*
7297	*Prussian blue*
7802	*mid-blue*
7404	*juniper green*
7424	*lime green*
7236	*dark brown*
7234	*light brown*
7927	*dark grey-blue*
7322	*pale grey-blue*
7323	*grey-blue*
7511	*raw umber*
7423	*deep yellow sand*
7525	*bronze*
7503	*yellow sand*
7406	*dark green*
7273	*dark grey*
7241	*light violet*
7253	*pink*
7255	*deep pink*
7300	*light grey*
7243	*dark violet*
7491	*beige*
7690	*kingfisher blue*
7271	*stone*
7426	*olive green*
(one skein each)	
blanc	*white*
(three skeins)	
7492	*pale yellow*
7301	*sky blue*
(seven skeins each)	

- Piece of 10-gauge double-thread canvas, 43 × 61cm (17 × 24in)
- Tapestry needles, sizes 22 and 26
- Piece of card, 28 × 45cm (11 × 17¾in)
- Strong thread

SIZE
The picture measures 28 × 45cm (11 × 17¾in).

TO MAKE THE PICTURE
Work the design in tent stitch, following the chart and using a single strand of thread in the size 22 needle. Leave spaces where indicated for the seagulls. Work these in tent stitch over every thread of the canvas, using the size 26 needle, thus getting 20 stitches to 2.5cm (1in). Carefully split the wool to obtain a narrower strand. Or use DMC's narrower Laine Zéphyr (introduced since I made this picture) in the following shades: 2415 (light grey), 2414 (dark grey) and 2100 (white). Or, if you prefer, you can simply omit the seagulls and fill in these areas with sky blue.

Block the completed work (see page 120). Mount it over the card (see page 121) and place it in a frame.

CHART FOR BEACH TENTS PICTURE

CHART FOR BIRDS

7301 sky blue

7802 mid-blue

7297 Prussian blue

7322 pale grey-blue

7323 grey-blue

7927 dark grey-blue

7690 kingfisher blue

7424 lime green

7404 juniper green

7406 dark green

7426 olive green

7491 beige

7451 pale flesh pink

7590 deep flesh pink

7492 pale yellow

7503 yellow sand

7423 deep yellow sand

7511 raw umber

7525 bronze

7234 light brown

7236 dark brown

7300 light grey

7271 stone

7273 dark grey

7241 light violet

7243 dark violet

7266 dark maroon

7226 maroon

7255 deep pink

7253 pink

blanc white

On the way to market.

FARM
Holiday Memories

FROM THE AGE OF SEVEN, *I spent the Easter holidays, too, in Wales. My mother would put me on the train with a label on my coat and tell the guard to be sure I got off at Newport. I used to love getting past the dingy houses of London and out into the country to see the lambs in the fields.*

My aunt and uncle's house backed on to fields and the River Usk. I'd awaken in the morning to the clucking of my aunt's hens and the farm cockerels, and would run to the window to see the mist creeping up from the river and the cows in the field behind the house.

I'd collect the warm, newly laid eggs for my aunt and eat one for breakfast. Ducks and geese roamed the fields behind the farmhouse, and would advance fiercely, honking and quacking, but run away as soon as one shouted back.

Farmyard Sampler

Rabbits, chicks and ducks scamper across this
sampler, designed for a child's bedroom.

MATERIALS

DMC stranded embroidery
cotton in the following
colours:

977	*orange*
962	*pink*
452	*grey*
471	*lime green*
502	*soft green*
blanc neige *white*	
(one skein each)	
792	*blue*
726	*yellow*
(two skeins each)	

● Piece of 11-count cream
easy-count Aida cloth,
46 × 38cm (18 × 15in)
● Tapestry needle, size 22
● Piece of card, 31 × 25cm
(12¼ × 10in)
● Strong thread

SIZE

The sampler measures
31 × 25cm (12¼ × 10in).

TO MAKE THE SAMPLER

Work the design in cross
stitch, following the chart
and using three strands of
thread.

Press the completed work.
Mount it over card (see page
121) and place it in a frame.

VARIATIONS

Any of the rows of animals
would work well across a
baby's bib or decorating a
toddler's dungarees or skirt.

+ = centre of design

792 blue   977 orange   452 grey   502 soft green

726 yellow   962 pink   471 lime green   blanc neige white

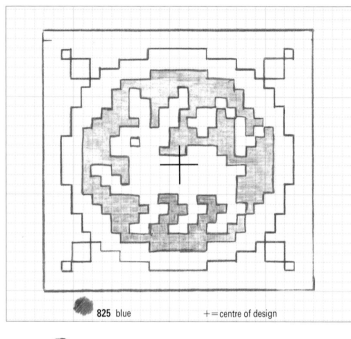

Rabbit Pincushion

This jolly rabbit pincushion would make a welcome present for someone who loves animals.

MATERIALS

DMC stranded embroidery cotton, one skein of the following colour:

825 *blue*

- Piece of 28-count white evenweave cloth, 18 × 10.5cm (7 × 4in)
- Tapestry needle, size 26
- Piece of 2.5cm (1in)-thick wadding, 18 × 10.5cm

(7 × 4in), plus another piece, 9 × 10.5cm (3½ × 4in)
- Small amount of pot-pourri

SIZE

The pincushion measures about 8 × 8cm (3 × 3in).

TO MAKE THE PINCUSHION

Fold the material in half across its width so that it measures 9 × 10.5cm (3½ × 4in). Work the design

825 blue   + = centre of design

on one half, beginning with the Holbein stitch outline (see page 117) and positioning the top line six fabric threads from the fold. Fill in with cross stitch. You can use either two or three strands of thread. Each square of the chart represents one stitch worked over *three* threads of the fabric.

Press the completed work, and make up the pincushion following the instructions on page 121.

VARIATION

The rabbit motif could be worked in cross stitch, on a plain background, and used to edge a child's curtains.

Collie Dog Paperweight

This alert collie, with one paw raised, ready to round up some sheep, fits neatly into a round glass paperweight.

MATERIALS

DMC stranded embroidery cotton, one skein each of the following colours:

3371	*dark brown*
839	*mid-brown*
433	*light brown*
écru	*cream*

● Piece of 16-count grey-green Aida cloth, 14 × 14cm ($5\frac{1}{2} \times 5\frac{1}{2}$in)

● Tapestry needle, size 24
● Round glass paperweight, 8.7cm ($3\frac{1}{2}$in) in diameter. The paperweight shown is available from DMC (see page 126) and is listed as item N857. Buy the paperweight first; if you cannot obtain one of this size, you will need to adjust the size of the embroidery accordingly.

SIZE

The finished design measures approximately 6cm ($2\frac{1}{2}$in) in diameter.

TO MAKE THE PAPERWEIGHT

Work the design in cross stitch, following the chart and using two strands of thread. Each square represents one stitch.

Press the completed work. Make up the paperweight following the instructions on page 124.

VARIATION

This design could also be made as a greetings card. For this you will need a card measuring 12 × 9cm ($4\frac{1}{2} \times 3\frac{1}{2}$in) (DMC N2501).

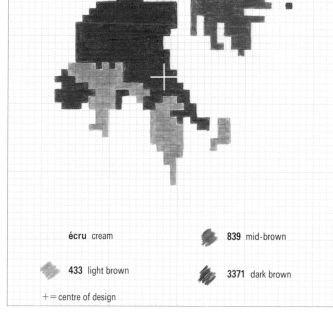

écru cream		**839** mid-brown
433 light brown		**3371** dark brown
+ = centre of design			

*𝒟*oggie scampers when I call,
   And has a heart to love us all.

Cats and Dogs, CHRISTINA ROSSETTI

Cow and Calf Picture

This picture would make a good present for anyone who loves the countryside and its animals.

*T*he friendly cow all red and white,
I love with all my heart:
She gives me cream with all her might,
To eat with apple tart.

And blown by all the winds that pass,
And wet by all the showers,
She walks among the meadow grass
And eats the meadow flowers.

The Cow, ROBERT LOUIS STEVENSON

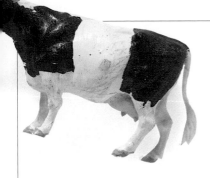

MATERIALS

DMC stranded embroidery cotton, one skein each of the following colours:

317	*dark grey*
712	*cream*
407	*brown*
502	*dark green*
3348	*light green*
931	*dark blue*
928	*pale blue*
950	*flesh pink*
648	*grey*
224	*pink*

● Piece of 14-count white Aida cloth, 23 × 26cm (9 × 10½in)

● Tapestry needle, size 24
● Piece of card, 14 × 10cm (5½ × 4in)
● Strong thread

SIZE

The picture measures 14 × 10cm (5½ × 4in).

TO MAKE THE PICTURE

Work the design in cross stitch, following the chart and using two strands of thread.

Press the completed work, mount it over the card (see page 121) and place it in a frame.

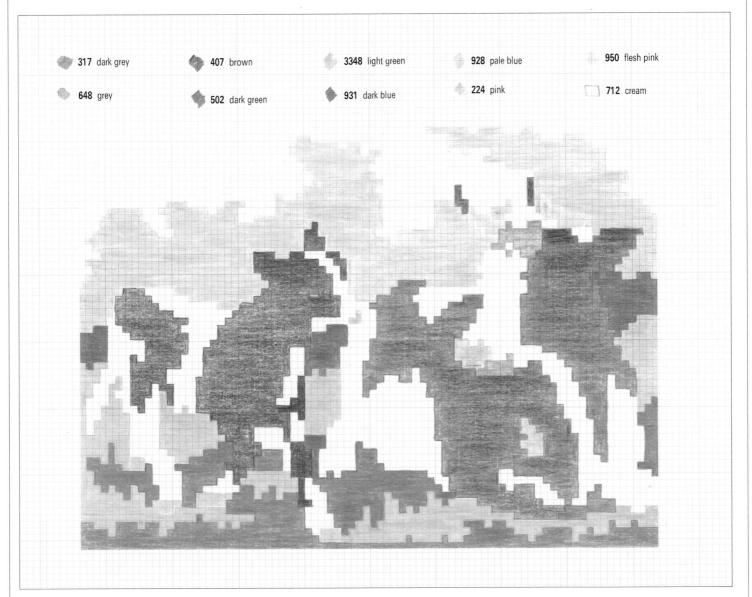

317 dark grey	**407** brown	**3348** light green	**928** pale blue	**950** flesh pink
648 grey	**502** dark green	**931** dark blue	**224** pink	**712** cream

Chicken and Chicks Card and Paperweight

This simple design can be used either for a greetings card or for a paperweight (making an ideal desk accessory for anyone who keeps chickens!).

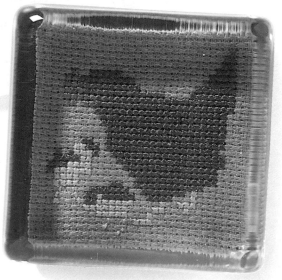

MATERIALS

DMC stranded embroidery cotton, one skein each of the following colours:

356 *pale red*	
413 *dark grey*	
726 *yellow*	

- Piece of 16-count olive green Aida cloth, 13 × 10cm (5 × 4in)
- Tapestry needle, size 24
- Greetings card for embroidery, 12 × 9cm (4½ × 3½in), with a circular opening 6.5cm (2½in) in diameter (DMC N2501)
or
- Glass paperweight, 6.2 × 6.2cm (2½ × 2½in). The paperweight shown is available from DMC (see page 126) and is listed as item N854. Buy the paperweight first; if you cannot obtain one of this size, you will need to adjust the size of the embroidery.

SIZE

The design measures 4.5cm (1¾in) in diameter.

TO MAKE THE CARD OR PAPERWEIGHT

Work the design in cross stitch, following the chart and using two strands of thread. Each square represents one stitch.

Press the completed work. Make up the card following the instructions on page 124. For the paperweight, also see instructions on page 124.

VARIATION

This motif could, instead, be worked in tent stitch on canvas, using tapestry wool, and framed as a small picture. Choose any colour you like for the background, which could be either round or square. (See the stranded cotton–tapestry wool colour conversion chart on page 127.)

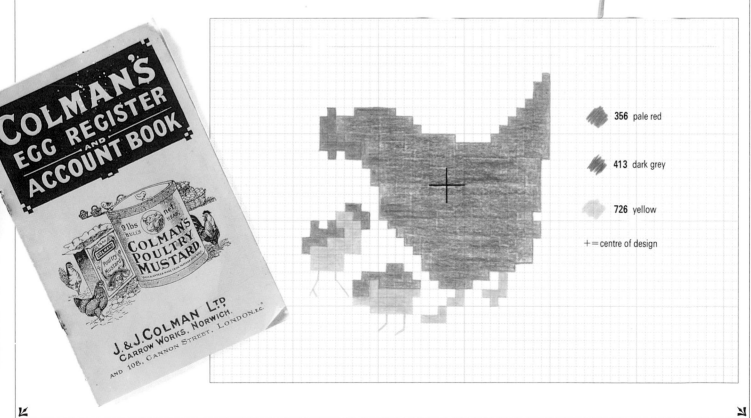

356 pale red

413 dark grey

726 yellow

+ = centre of design

CHART ON PAGES 50–1

Pigs Cushion

A plump mother sow and her piglets enjoy the sunshine in this farmyard-scene cushion. The warm colours of the wool are complemented by the soft brown velvet border.

CHART ON PAGES 52–3

Sheep Cushion

This pastoral scene of young lambs with their
mother makes an appealing cushion cover – worked,
appropriately, in wool.

*O*n the grassy banks,
Lambkins at their pranks.

Lambkins,
CHRISTINA ROSSETTI

CHART FOR PIGS CUSHION

 7170 pale pink

 7460 mid-pink

7543 dark pink

7390 light brown

7415 dark brown

7321 grey

7271 beige

7273 dark grey

7422 light green

7376 mid-green

7427 dark green

7703 blue-green

7587 pale blue

MATERIALS

DMC tapestry wool (Laine Colbert) in the following colours:

7587 *pale blue*	
7273 *dark grey*	
7703 *blue-green*	
7427 *dark green*	
7543 *dark pink*	
(one skein each)	
7376 *mid-green*	
7422 *light green*	
(two skeins each)	
7460 *mid-pink*	
7321 *grey*	
7415 *dark brown*	
7271 *beige*	
(three skeins each)	
7390 *light brown*	
7170 *pale pink*	
(four skeins each)	

● Piece of 10-gauge white single-thread or interlock canvas, 56 × 56cm (22 × 22in)
● Tapestry needle, size 22
● Piece of velvet, or other furnishing fabric, 49 × 49cm (19½ × 19½in)
● Four strips of the same fabric, each 49 × 8.5cm (19½ × 3½in)
● 2.2m (2½yd) of 1cm (⅜in)-diameter furnishing braid
● Cushion pad, 45 × 45cm (18 × 18in)

SIZE

The design measures 36 × 36cm (14 × 14in); the completed cushion, 45 × 45cm (18 × 18in).

TO MAKE THE CUSHION

Work the design in tent stitch, following the chart, using one strand of thread.

Block the completed work (see page 120). Make it up into a cushion following the instructions on page 122.

MATERIALS

DMC tapestry wool (Laine Colbert) in the following colours:

7262	*mauve*
7870	*mid-green*
7221	*dark pink*
7451	*pink*
7322	*blue-green*
7335	*dark green*
7703	*green*
(one skein each)	
7232	*brown*
7500	*pale pink*
7361	*lime green*
7510	*light grey*
(two skeins each)	
7587	*sky blue*
7492	*yellow*
(three skeins each)	
écru	*cream*
7704	*light green*
(four skeins each)	

● Piece of 10-gauge single-thread or interlock canvas, 56 × 56cm (22 × 22in)
● Tapestry needle, size 22
● Piece of velvet, or other furnishing fabric, 49 × 49cm (19½ × 19½in)
● Four strips of the same fabric, each 49 × 8.5cm (19½ × 3½in)
● 2.2m (2½yd) of 1cm (⅜in)-diameter furnishing braid
● Cushion pad, 45 × 45cm (18 × 18in)

SIZE

The design measures 36 × 36cm (14 × 14in); the completed cushion, 45 × 45cm (18 × 18in).

TO MAKE THE CUSHION

Work the design in tent stitch, following the chart, using one strand of thread.

Block the completed work (see page 120). Make it up into a cushion (see instructions on page 122).

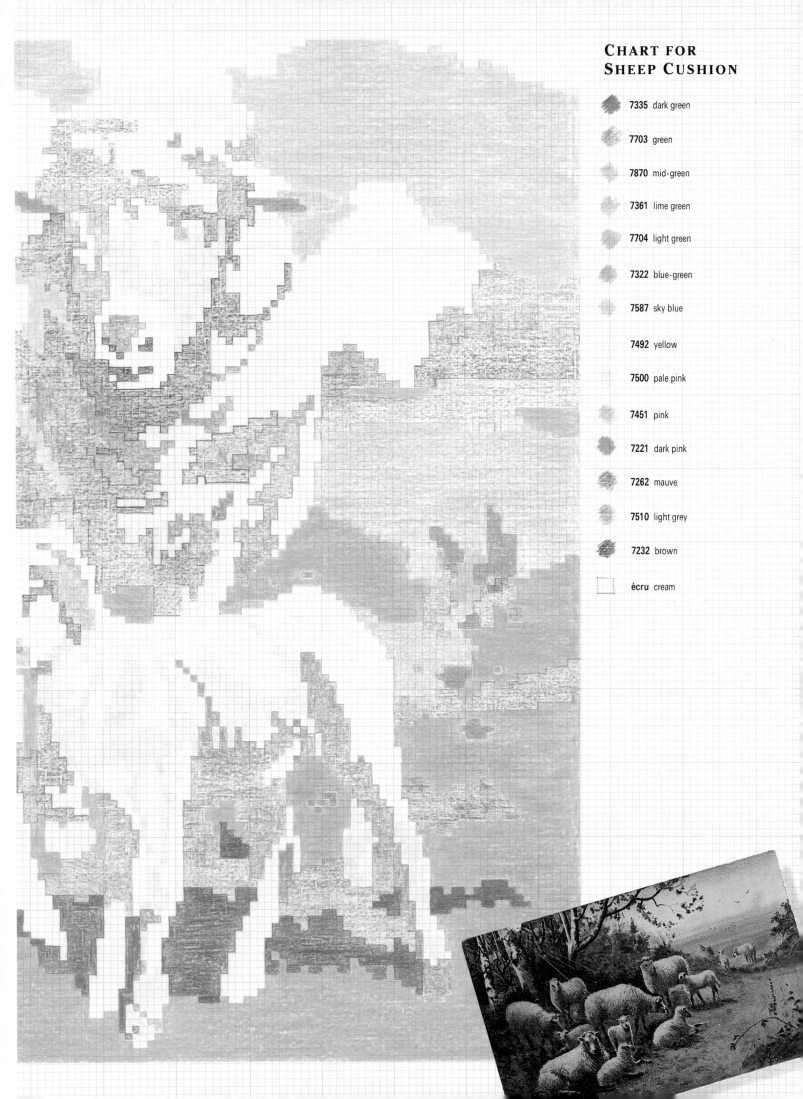

CHART FOR SHEEP CUSHION

	7335	dark green
	7703	green
	7870	mid-green
	7361	lime green
	7704	light green
	7322	blue-green
	7587	sky blue
	7492	yellow
	7500	pale pink
	7451	pink
	7221	dark pink
	7262	mauve
	7510	light grey
	7232	brown
	écru	cream

CHART ON PAGES 56–7

Rabbits Cushion

No one has to urge rabbits to eat their greens! Here
they are tucking into some salad.

CHART ON PAGES 58–9

Geese Cushion

Papa Gander looks on serenely while Mama Goose
issues instructions to her lively goslings.

*T*hese sturdy geese are fat and fine,
They march like soldiers in a line.
They cackle when they want to talk,
And don't they waddle when they walk.

ANON

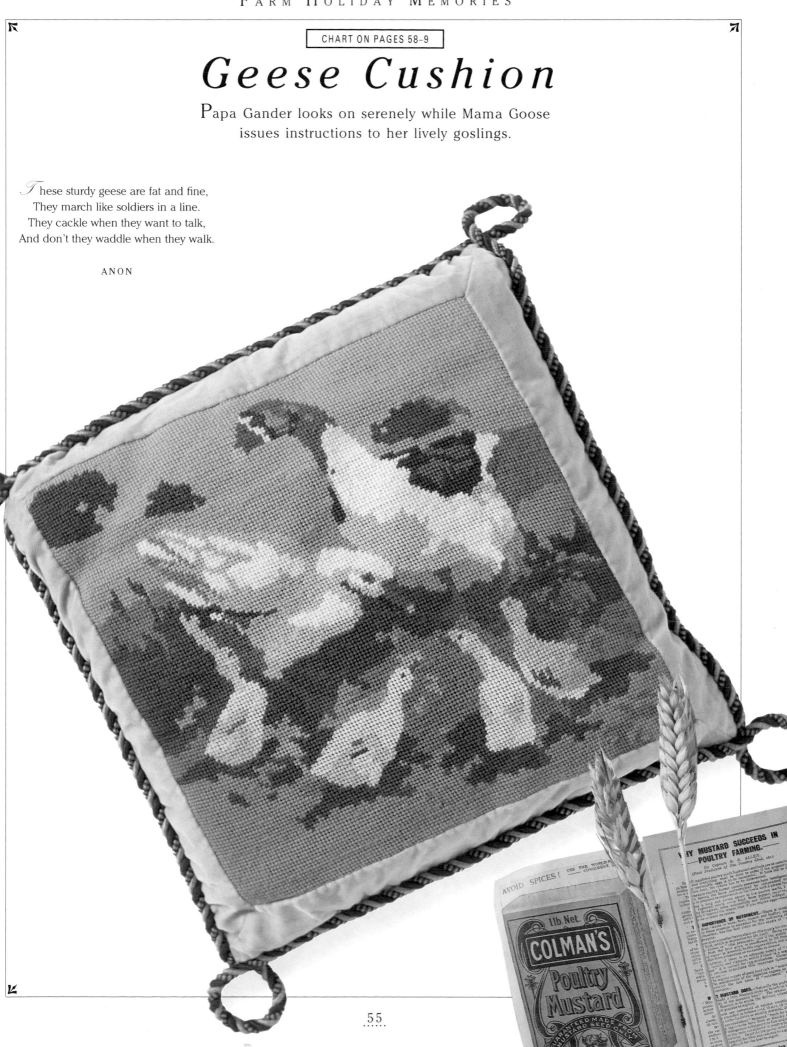

CHART FOR
RABBITS CUSHION

- **7327** dark blue-green
- **7404** mid-green
- **7326** mid-blue-green
- **7323** light blue-green
- **7301** sky blue
- **7280** pale beige
- **7510** fawn
- **7622** dark grey
- **7234** light brown
- **7236** dark brown
- **7176** orange
- **7501** pale yellow
- **7200** pink
- **blanc** white

MATERIALS

DMC tapestry wool (Laine Colbert) in the following colours:

7200	*pink*
7327	*dark blue-green*
7176	*orange*
7301	*sky blue*
(one skein each)	
7326	*mid-blue-green*
7234	*light brown*
7510	*fawn*
7622	*dark grey*
7323	*light blue-green*
(two skeins each)	
7404	*mid-green*
7236	*dark brown*
blanc	*white*
(three skeins each)	
7501	*pale yellow*
(four skeins)	
7280	*pale beige*
(five skeins)	

● Piece of 10-gauge white single-thread or interlock canvas, 56 × 56cm (22 × 22in)
● Tapestry needle, size 22
● Piece of furnishing fabric, 49 × 49cm (19½ × 19½in)
● Four strips of the same fabric, 49 × 8.5cm (19½ × 3½in)
● 2.2m (2½yd) of 1cm (⅜in)-diameter furnishing braid
● Cushion pad, 45 × 45cm (18 × 18in)

SIZE

The design measures 36 × 36cm (14 × 14in); the completed cushion, 45 × 45cm (18 × 18in).

TO MAKE THE CUSHION

Work the design in tent stitch, following the chart, using one strand of thread.

Block the completed work (see page 120). Make it up into a cushion following the instructions on page 122.

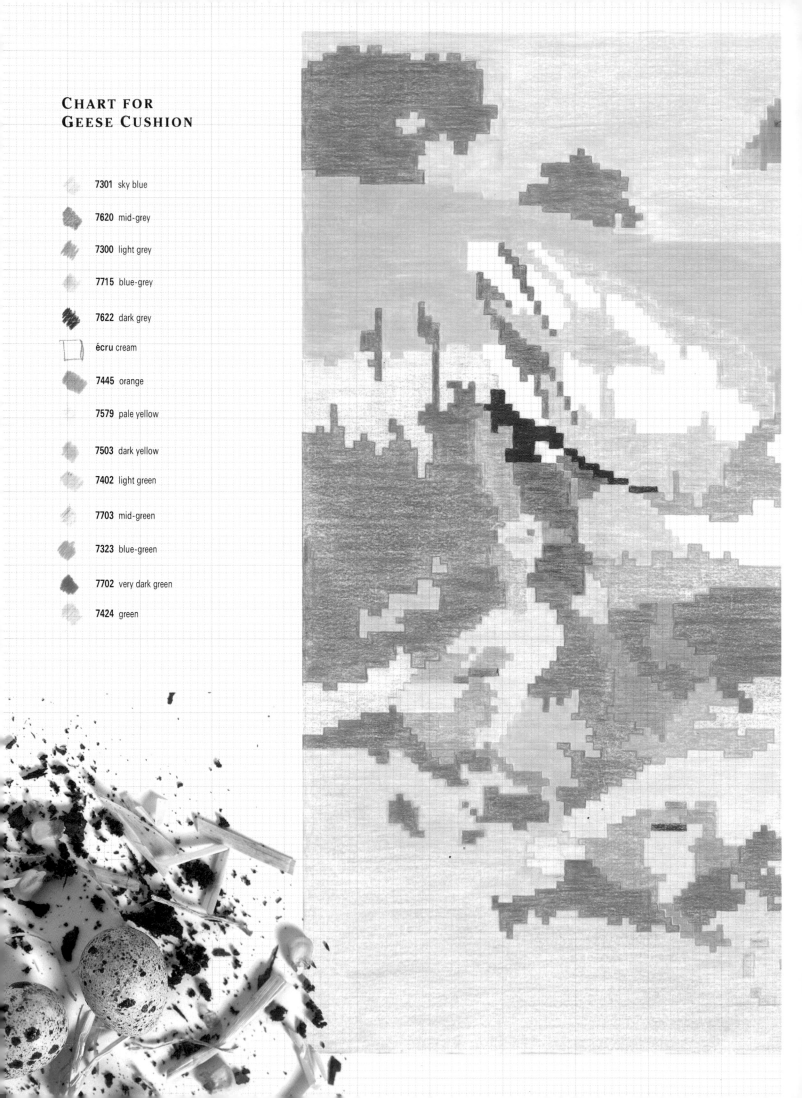

7301 sky blue

7620 mid-grey

7300 light grey

7715 blue-grey

7622 dark grey

écru cream

7445 orange

7579 pale yellow

7503 dark yellow

7402 light green

7703 mid-green

7323 blue-green

7702 very dark green

7424 green

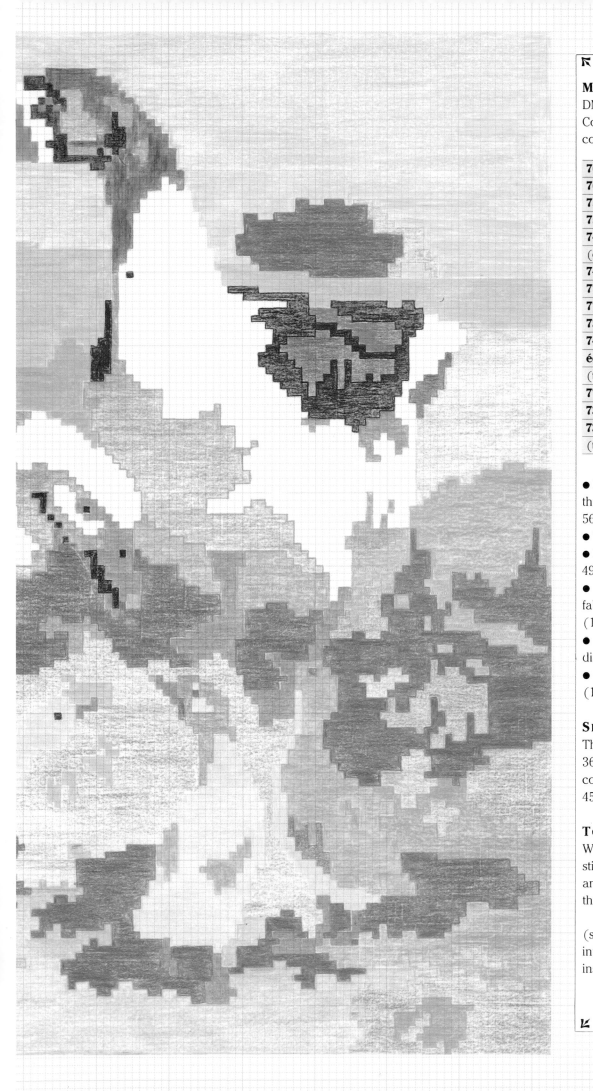

MATERIALS

DMC tapestry wool (Laine Colbert) in the following colours:

7620 *mid-grey*	
7622 *dark grey*	
7579 *pale yellow*	
7503 *dark yellow*	
7445 *orange*	
(one skein each)	
7402 *light green*	
7703 *mid-green*	
7702 *very dark green*	
7323 *blue-green*	
7424 *green*	
écru *cream*	
(two skeins each)	
7715 *blue-grey*	
7300 *light grey*	
7301 *sky blue*	
(three skeins each)	

● Piece of 10-gauge single-thread or interlock canvas, 56 × 56cm (22 × 22in)
● Tapestry needle, size 22
● Piece of furnishing fabric, 49 × 49cm (19½ × 19½in)
● Four strips of the same fabric, 49 × 8.5cm (19½ × 3½in)
● 2.2m (2½yd) of 1cm (⅜in)-diameter furnishing braid
● Cushion pad, 45 × 45cm (18 × 18in)

SIZE

The design measures 36 × 36cm (14 × 14in); the completed cushion, 45 × 45cm (18 × 18in).

TO MAKE THE CUSHION

Work the design in tent stitch, following the chart and using a single strand of thread.

Block the completed work (see page 120). Make it up into a cushion following the instructions on page 122.

Duck and Drake Card

A colourful drake steps out with a snowy duck and her ducklings in this appealing design for a greetings card.

MATERIALS

DMC stranded embroidery cotton, one skein each of the following colours:

501	*green*
356	*terra cotta*
676	*yellow*
écru	*cream*
839	*brown*
5200	*white*

● Piece of 14-count Confederate grey Aida cloth, 13 × 10cm (5 × 4in)
● Tapestry needle, size 24
● Greetings card for embroidery, 12 × 9cm (4½ × 3½in), with oval opening, 7.5 × 5cm (3 × 2in) (DMC N2500)

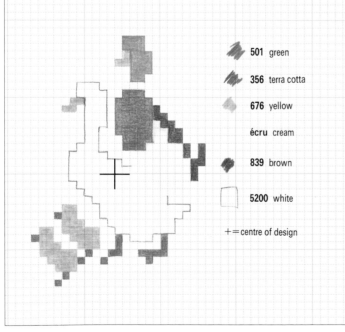

501	green
356	terra cotta
676	yellow
écru	cream
839	brown
5200	white

+ = centre of design

SIZE

The design measures 6 × 4.2cm (2½ × 1¾in).

TO MAKE THE CARD

Work the design in cross stitch, following the chart and using two strands of thread. Each square represents one stitch.

Press the completed work. Insert it in the card following the instructions on page 124.

VARIATIONS

This design could be used in all sorts of other ways – for a paperweight or a small picture, for example, perhaps worked on single-thread evenweave at a larger scale. The duck and ducklings could be repeated to make an attractive border design or they could be sewn as a motif on a child's pillowcase or blouse.

CHART ON PAGES 62–3

Goats Cushion

The nanny goat sits contentedly in the spring
sunshine watching her lively kids have a playful
butting match.

MATERIALS

DMC tapestry wool (Laine Colbert) in the following colours:

7326	*dark blue-green*
7492	*yellow*
7390	*beige*
7713	*dark grey*
7335	*dark green*
7294	*dark blue*
7200	*pink*
7618	*mid-grey*
(one skein each)	
7323	*light blue-green*
7704	*light green*
7333	*mid-green*
7422	*lime green*
(two skeins each)	
7587	*sky blue*
7715	*light grey*
blanc	*white*
(three skeins each)	

● Piece of 10-gauge single-thread or interlock canvas, 56 × 56cm (22 × 22in)
● Tapestry needle, size 22
● Piece of velvet, or other furnishing fabric, 49 × 49cm (19½ × 19½in)
● Four strips of the same fabric, each 49 × 8.5cm (19½ × 3½in)
● 2.2m (2½yd) of 1cm (⅜in)-diameter furnishing braid
● Cushion pad, 45 × 45cm (18 × 18in)

SIZE

The design measures 36 × 36cm (14 × 14in); the completed cushion, 45 × 45cm (18 × 18in).

TO MAKE THE CUSHION

Work the design in tent stitch, following the chart, using one strand of thread.

Block the completed work (see page 120). Make it up into a cushion following the instructions on page 122.

	7713	dark grey
	7618	mid-grey
	7715	light grey
	7587	sky blue
	7294	dark blue
	7323	light blue-green
	7704	light green
	7422	lime green
	7326	dark blue-green
	7335	dark green
	7333	mid-green
	7390	beige
	7492	yellow
	7200	pink
	blanc	white

FLORAL
Memories

FLOWERS HAVE ALWAYS BEEN *very important
to me. My childhood favourite was the
snapdragon. I'd sit for ages watching bees land
on the lower lip, crawl inside and then back out,
covered in pollen.*
*There were plenty of flowers in London, where I spent
most of my childhood. Highgate Woods were full of
bluebells in May, and there were wood anemones.
The cherry trees in our road blossomed in spring, and
we had flowers in our garden.*
*On holidays in Wales the profusion of wild flowers
was intoxicating. I loved walking through fields of
buttercups and poppies in summer, and smelling the
heavy scent of honeysuckle in the hedgerows.*
*At my cousins' house we would make dams in the
brook and float flower heads on the water. We'd
make fairy houses out of lumps of moss and small
gardens with wild flowers, which we pushed down
into the moss.*

Morning Glory Sampler

For me, the morning glory epitomizes high summer – its brilliant blue tones echoing the clear blue sky, the deeper purple shades evoking a warm summer evening.

MATERIALS

DMC stranded embroidery cotton, one skein each of the following colours:

| 809 *blue* |
| 926 *green* |
| 340 *lilac* |

- Piece of 14-count white Aida cloth, 35 × 30cm (14 × 12in)
- Tapestry needle, size 24
- Piece of card, 25 × 19cm (10 × 7½in)
- Strong thread

SIZE

The sampler measures 25 × 19cm (10 × 7½in).

TO MAKE THE SAMPLER

Work the design in cross stitch, following the chart and using two strands of thread. Each square represents one stitch.

Press the completed work, mount it over the card (see page 121) and place it in a frame.

VARIATIONS

The border could be used on Aida band and made into a bookmark or edging for a pillowcase. Or the design could be embroidered straight on to a blouse. The flower in the centre could be used for a greetings card.

809 blue   **926** green   **340** lilac

+ = centre of design

Lavender Sachet

This little sachet filled with lavender and embroidered with a sprig of the plant itself will keep linens smelling sweet.

MATERIALS

DMC stranded embroidery cotton, one skein each of the following colours:

340	light mauve
3746	dark mauve
927	light green
926	dark green

● Piece of 27-count white cotton evenweave cloth 9 × 22cm (3½ × 8¾in)
● Tapestry needle, size 26
● Dried lavender

SIZE

The sachet measures about 7 × 10cm (2¾ × 4in).

TO MAKE THE SACHET

Work the design in cross stitch, following the chart. Each square represents one stitch. Position the lowest stitch of the design 1.5cm (⅝in) in from one short edge, and centre the motif as indicated on the chart. Use two strands of thread.

Turn under 1cm (⅜in) along all four edges; press. Fold the fabric in half across the middle. Using two strands of 340, work blanket stitch (see page 117) around all four edges, leaving a small opening in one side. Fill this with the lavender, then complete the stitching.

I picked a bunch of lavender
To scent my dollies' clothes.
I wrapped it round with ribbons
And tied it up with bows.

My dollies were so pleased
To find their clothes all smelling sweet
I put some more in a little bag
And embroidered it so neat.

ANON

340 light mauve

927 light green

3746 dark mauve

926 dark green

+ = centre of design

CHART ON PAGES 72–3

Flowers in Round Vase Cushion

A profusion of blooms in a blue vase makes a design that works equally well for a cushion and for a picture (see page 74). To enhance the Victorian look of the cushion I used antique velvet and tassels when making it up.

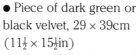

MATERIALS

DMC tapestry wool (Laine Colbert) in the following colours:

7920	*light red*
7184	*dark red*
7200	*light pink*
7221	*dark pink*
7193	*salmon*
7244	*mauve*
7262	*lilac*
7266	*dark lilac*
7316	*light blue*
7318	*dark blue*
7690	*light green*
7926	*dark green*
7745	*pale yellow*
7727	*deep yellow*
7506	*yellow ochre*
7758	*wine red*
(1 skein each)	
7925	*very dark green*
(5 skeins)	

● Piece of 10-gauge white single-thread or interlock canvas, 46 × 56cm (18 × 22in)
● Tapestry needle, size 22

● Piece of dark green or black velvet, 29 × 39cm (11½ × 15½in)
● 1.6m (1¾yd) of 1cm (⅜in)-diameter braid
● Four tassels
● Cushion pad, 35 × 35cm (14 × 14in); a feather pad squashed down to fit. Or make a rectangular pad from calico and polyester filling to fit this shape.

SIZE

The cushion measures 35 × 25cm (14 × 10in).

TO MAKE THE CUSHION

Work the design in tent stitch, following the chart and using a single strand of thread.

Block the completed work (see page 120). Make up the cushion (see page 122).

CHART FOR CUSHION AND PICTURE

CUSHION	PICTURE	
TAPESTRY WOOL	STRANDED EMBROIDERY COTTON	
7758	902	wine red
7184	817	dark red
7920	350	light red
7221	224	dark pink
7193	760	salmon
7200	225	light pink
7244	340	mauve
7262	3042	lilac
7266	3740	dark lilac
7316	798	light blue
7318	797	dark blue
7690	926	light green
7926	3768	dark green
7745	727	pale yellow
7727	726	deep yellow
7506	729	yellow ochre
very dark green 7925	écru	cream

72

CUSHION EDGE

PICTURE EDGE

Flowers in Round Vase Picture

Here the design for the cushion on page 70 is interpreted in stranded cotton with a cream-coloured background.

MATERIALS

DMC stranded embroidery cotton in the following colours:

350	*light red*
817	*dark red*
902	*wine red*
225	*light pink*
224	*dark pink*
760	*salmon*
340	*mauve*
3042	*lilac*
3740	*dark lilac*
798	*light blue*
797	*dark blue*
926	*light green*
3768	*dark green*
727	*pale yellow*
726	*deep yellow*
729	*yellow ochre*
(1 skein each)	
écru	*cream*
(5 skeins)	

- Piece of 14-count white Aida cloth, 36 × 43cm (14 × 17in)
- Tapestry needle, size 24
- Piece of card, 20 × 28cm (8 × 11in)
- Strong thread

SIZE

The picture measures 20 × 28cm (8 × 11in).

TO MAKE THE PICTURE

Work the design in cross stitch, following the chart on pages 72–3 and using two strands of thread. Each square represents one stitch. Note that the écru background of the picture extends for an additional six stitches beyond the cushion chart on all four sides.

Press the completed embroidery, mount it over the card (see page 121) and place it in a frame.

VARIATIONS

You could eliminate the background stitching, leaving the fabric exposed. (When working a design in this way, you must first centre it on the fabric; see page 118.)

You could reduce the size of the picture by working it on 18-count Aida, which would make it approximately 16 × 22cm (6¼ × 8½in).

Teesdale Violet Pendant

The pretty, delicate flowers of the Teesdale violet are a favourite of mine, and a perfect motif for a pendant.

TO MAKE THE PENDANT

Work the design in cross stitch, following the chart and using one strand of thread. One square represents one stitch, worked over one fabric thread. Work the veins on the leaves in backstitch, using 501.

Press the completed work. Dismantle the pendant. Position the plastic piece over the design, and draw around it. Cut around the line. Replace the plastic in the frame, and lay the design face down on top. Lay the pendant face down on a soft cloth, and place the filler card on top. Using a small coin, carefully roll the slit tags inwards over the card to hold everything in place. Slip the locket over the chain.

VARIATIONS

The design could be worked on a napkin, handkerchief or bookmark, for example, or on Aida for a card with an oval opening. It could also be used for a little picture, perhaps worked in tent stitch on canvas, using wool. (See the colour conversion chart on page 127.)

MATERIALS

DMC stranded embroidery cotton, one skein each of the following colours:

502	mid-green
501	dark green
3347	bright green
3363	leaf green
794	pale blue
793	mid-blue
792	dark blue

● Piece of 27-count *eau-de-nil* evenweave cloth, 8 × 6cm (3 × 2½in)
● Tapestry needle, size 26
● Oval pendant for embroidery. The pendant shown is available from DMC and is listed as item N860.

SIZE

The design measures 3.7 × 2.8cm (1⅜ × 1⅛in).

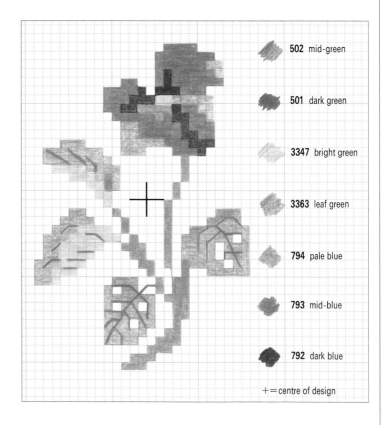

	502 mid-green
	501 dark green
	3347 bright green
	3363 leaf green
	794 pale blue
	793 mid-blue
	792 dark blue

+ = centre of design

Floral Bookmark

Bright little blossoms make a charming theme for a bookmark to give to someone special – or to keep for yourself!

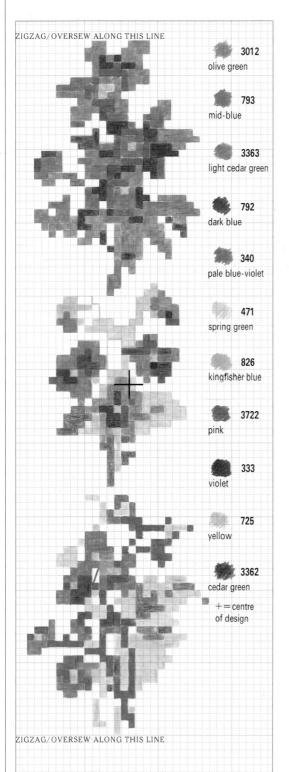

3012
olive green

793
mid-blue

3363
light cedar green

792
dark blue

340
pale blue-violet

471
spring green

826
kingfisher blue

3722
pink

333
violet

725
yellow

3362
cedar green

+ = centre of design

ZIGZAG/OVERSEW ALONG THIS LINE

MATERIALS

DMC stranded embroidery cotton, one skein each of the following colours:

3012	olive green
3363	light cedar green
3362	cedar green
725	yellow
333	violet
3722	pink
826	kingfisher blue
471	spring green
340	pale blue-violet
792	dark blue
793	mid-blue

● Piece of 15-count, 5cm (2in)-wide Aida band, 22cm (8½in) long
● Tapestry needle, size 24
● Piece of thin lining fabric, 6 × 18.5cm (2¼ × 7¼in)

SIZE

The design measures 16.5cm (6½in) long.

TO MAKE THE BOOKMARK

Work the design in cross stitch, following the chart and using two strands of thread. Each square represents one stitch.

Press the completed work. Apply the lining and finish the ends of the Aida band following the instructions on page 121.

Rose Greetings Card

Whatever the message – 'Happy Birthday', 'Get Well Soon', 'I Love You' – a rose says it beautifully.

MATERIALS

DMC stranded embroidery cotton, one skein each of the following colours:

502	*light green*
501	*dark green*
778	*pale pink*
316	*deep pink*
744	*yellow*

● Piece of 14-count cream Aida cloth, 14 × 12cm (5½ × 4½in)
● Tapestry needle, size 24
● Greetings card for embroidery, 12 × 9cm (4½ × 3½in), with oval opening, 7.5 × 5cm (3 × 2in) (DMC N2500)

SIZE

The design measures 6.5 × 4cm (2½ × 1½in).

TO MAKE THE CARD

Work the design in cross stitch, following the chart and using two strands of thread. Each square represents one stitch.

Press the completed work. Insert it in the card following the instructions on page 124.

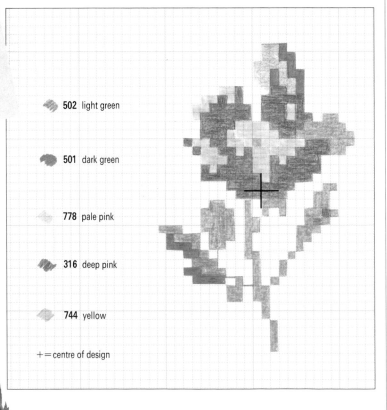

	502	light green
	501	dark green
	778	pale pink
	316	deep pink
	744	yellow

+ = centre of design

CHART ON PAGES 80–1

Flowers in Tall Vase Cushion

Masses of blossoms filling a vase are a perennially
popular theme in embroidery. I've placed these
against a dark blue background to set off their warm,
bright colours.

CHART FOR FLOWERS IN TALL VASE CUSHION

MATERIALS

DMC tapestry wool (Laine Colbert) in the following colours:

7260	*pale lilac-pink*
7200	*pale pink*
7221	*mid-pink*
7133	*light bright pink*
7804	*dark bright pink*
7226	*dark pink*
7244	*light violet*
7266	*dark violet*
7078	*pale yellow*
7726	*deep yellow*
7323	*blue-green*
7426	*dark olive green*
7373	*pale olive green*
7384	*grass green*
(one skein each)	
7304	*light blue*
7306	*mid-blue*
blanc	*white*
(two skeins each)	
7288	*Prussian blue*
(nine skeins)	
For the twisted cord, one skein each of	
7288	*Prussian blue*
7930	*lighter Prussian blue*
7384	*grass green*

● Piece of 10-gauge white single-thread or interlock canvas, 46 × 48cm (18 × 19in)
● Piece of velvet or other furnishing fabric, 34 × 37cm (13½ × 14½in)
● Tapestry needle, size 22
● Cushion pad, 35 × 35cm (14 × 14in); squash to fit. Or make your own cushion pad 32 × 35cm (12½ × 14in).

SIZE

The cushion measures approximately 30 × 33cm (12 × 13in).

TO MAKE THE CUSHION

Work the design in tent stitch, following the chart and using one strand of thread.

Block the completed work (see page 120). Make a twisted cord (see page 123), and make up the cushion following the instructions on page 122.

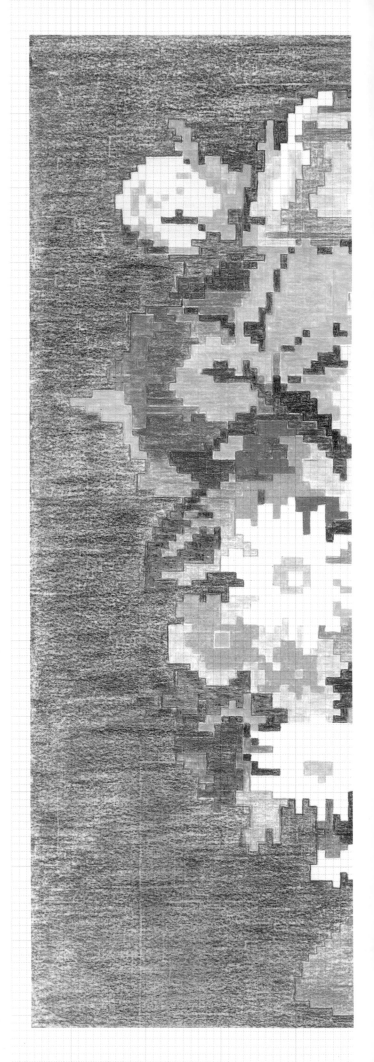

7200 pale pink

7133 light bright pink

7804 dark bright pink

7221 mid-pink

7226 dark pink

7260 pale lilac-pink

7244 light violet

7266 dark violet

7078 pale yellow

7726 deep yellow

7323 blue-green

7384 grass green

7373 pale olive green

7426 dark olive green

7304 light blue

7306 mid-blue

7288 Prussian blue

blanc white

Wild Pansy Brooch Cushion

Delicate wild pansies adorn this brooch cushion – a useful as well as decorative object for the dressing table. I used antique velvet, braid and tassels for the cushion.

MATERIALS

DMC stranded embroidery cotton, one skein each of the following colours:

726	yellow
3740	violet
blanc neige	white
502	green
503	light green
523	light olive green

- Piece of 14-count pink Aida cloth, 15 × 15cm (6 × 6in)
- Two pieces of fabric, such as velvet, each 20 × 20cm (8 × 8in)
- Tapestry needle, size 24
- 40cm (16in) of 5mm ($\frac{1}{4}$in)-wide braid
- Four tassels
- Polyester filling
- Small amount of dried lavender (optional)

SIZE

The design measures 7.5 × 5.5cm (3 × 2$\frac{1}{4}$in); the completed cushion, 20 × 20cm (7$\frac{3}{4}$ × 7$\frac{3}{4}$in).

TO MAKE THE CUSHION

Work the design in cross stitch, following the chart and using two strands of thread. Each square represents one stitch.

Press the completed work. Trim the fabric evenly to measure 10cm (4in) square. Turn under and press 5mm ($\frac{1}{4}$in) on all edges. Pin and tack [baste] the embroidery to the centre of one fabric square. Slipstitch it in place, then sew braid around the edges, joining the ends.

Join the front and back as described on page 122. Insert stuffing and pot-pourri, if desired, then slipstitch the gap to close. Sew a tassel to each corner.

VARIATION

The design could be used as a small picture in an oval frame, worked on whatever count of Aida cloth or evenweave you prefer.

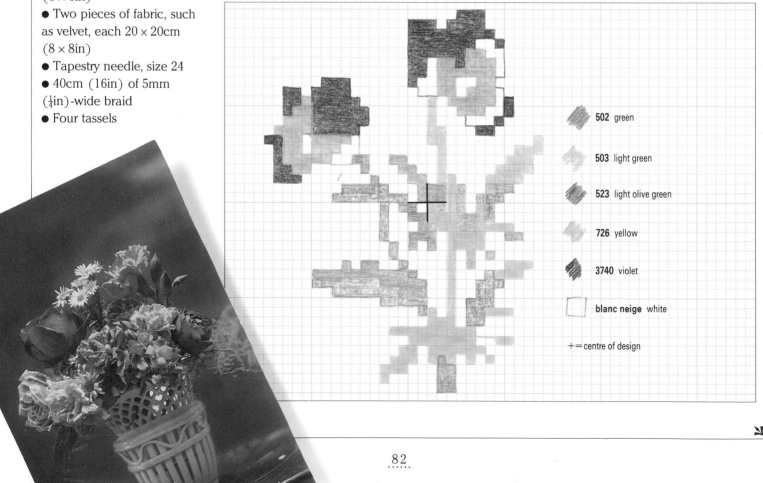

- 502 green
- 503 light green
- 523 light olive green
- 726 yellow
- 3740 violet
- blanc neige white

+ = centre of design

Iris Pincushion

A delicate iris in Assisi work adorns this scented pincushion.

MATERIALS

DMC stranded embroidery cotton, one skein of the following colour:

221 *deep red*

● Piece of 28-count cream evenweave cloth, 18 × 10.5cm (7 × 4in)
● Tapestry needle, size 26
● Piece of 2.5cm (1in)-thick wadding, 18 × 10.5cm (7 × 4in), plus another piece, 9 × 10.5cm (3½ × 4in)
● Small amount of pot-pourri

SIZE

The pincushion measures about 8 × 8cm (3 × 3in).

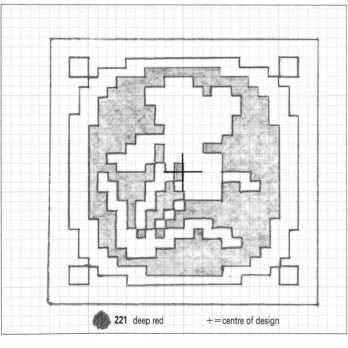

221 deep red   + = centre of design

TO MAKE THE PINCUSHION

Fold the material in half across its width so that it measures 9 × 10.5cm (3½ × 4in). Work the design on one half, beginning with the Holbein stitch outline (see page 117) and positioning the top line six fabric threads from the fold. Fill in with cross stitch. You can use either two or three strands of thread. Each square of the chart represents one stitch worked over *three* threads of the fabric.

Press the completed work, and make up the pincushion following the instructions on page 121.

VARIATION

This iris motif could be repeated to make a border pattern of Assisi work on a guest towel.

Pansy Paperweight

I love pansies, and I think their cheerful little faces make a good design to have on one's desk.

MATERIALS

DMC stranded embroidery cotton, one skein each of the following colours:

676	*yellow*
3041	*dark mauve*
3042	*light mauve*
841	*brown*
932	*blue*
356	*rust*

● Piece of 22-count cream Hardanger cloth, 13 × 13cm (5 × 5in)
● Tapestry needle, size 26
● Square glass paperweight, 6.2 × 6.2cm (2½ × 2½in). The paperweight shown is available from DMC (see page 126) and is listed as item N854. Buy the paperweight first; if you cannot obtain one of this size, the design will fit into the N857 8.7cm (3½in) round paperweight or the N858 8.7cm (3½in) fluted paperweight.

SIZE

The finished design measures approximately 5 × 5cm (2 × 2in).

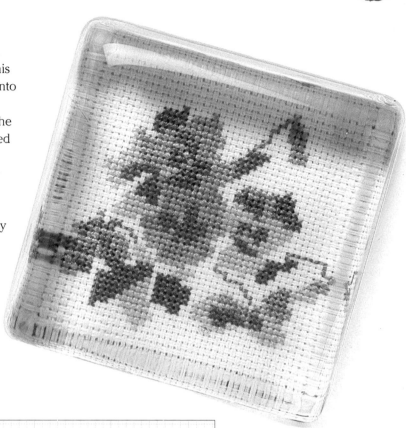

	3041	dark mauve
	3042	light mauve
	932	blue
	356	rust
	841	brown
	676	yellow
+	= centre of design	

TO MAKE THE PAPERWEIGHT

Work the design in cross stitch, following the chart and using two strands of thread. Each square represents one stitch.

Press the completed work. Make up the paperweight following the instructions on page 124.

VARIATIONS

This design could be used for a greetings card. It could also be worked on 14-, 16- or 18-count Aida as a small picture or the centre of a brooch cushion.

Floral Birth Sampler

A happy event deserves a special commemoration. Stitch this sampler, inserting your own good news within the floral border.

MATERIALS

DMC stranded embroidery cotton, one skein each of the following colours:

727	*pale yellow*
726	*mid-yellow*
725	*dark yellow*

341	*light blue*
793	*dark blue*
368	*light green*
501	*dark green*
948	*pale flesh pink*
950	*dark flesh pink*
3354	*pale pink*
3733	*deep pink*

- Piece of 14-count white easy-count Aida cloth, 40 × 32cm (16 × 12½in)
- Tapestry needle, size 24
- Graph paper
- Piece of card, 26 × 17cm (10¼ × 6¾in)
- Strong thread

SIZE

The sampler measures 26 × 17cm (10¼ × 6¾in).

TO MAKE THE SAMPLER

First work the border and baby design in cross stitch, following the chart and using two strands of thread. Each square represents one stitch.

Next write down the information appropriate to your sampler and chart it on the graph paper. (See page 125 for instructions on how to chart lettering.) Indicate the position of the border and the babies on your own chart, to be sure of getting the positioning right.

Following your own chart, work the lettering in cross stitch, again using two strands of thread.

Press the completed embroidery, mount it over the card (see page 121) and place it in a frame.

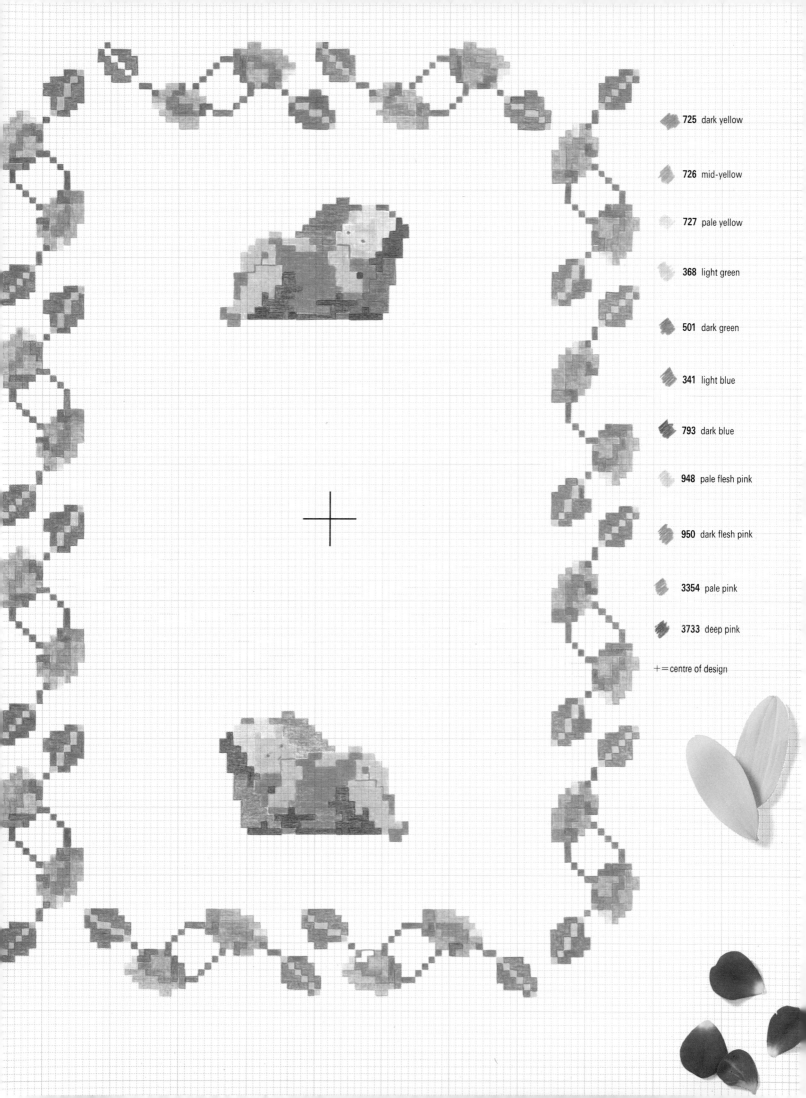

725 dark yellow

726 mid-yellow

727 pale yellow

368 light green

501 dark green

341 light blue

793 dark blue

948 pale flesh pink

950 dark flesh pink

3354 pale pink

3733 deep pink

+ = centre of design

Flower Borders

Here is a selection of borders that can be used in a variety of ways. You could work them on 5cm (2in)-wide Aida band to make bookmarks, or you could embroider them directly on to linens or garments.

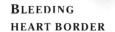

BLEEDING HEART BORDER
DMC stranded embroidery cotton in the following colours:

501	*green*
961	*pink*
3042	*lilac*

BLUE AND LILAC FLOWER BORDER
DMC stranded embroidery cotton in the following colours:

3042	*lilac*
792	*blue*
3768	*green*

PINK AND YELLOW FLOWER BORDER
DMC stranded embroidery cotton in the following colours:

726	*yellow*
776	*pink*
502	*green*

POINSETTIA BORDER
DMC stranded embroidery cotton in the following colours:

817	*deep red*
350	*mid-red*
501	*sage green*

SWAGGED BORDER
DMC stranded embroidery cotton in the following colours:

347	*red*
3712	*terra cotta*
3768	*grey-green*

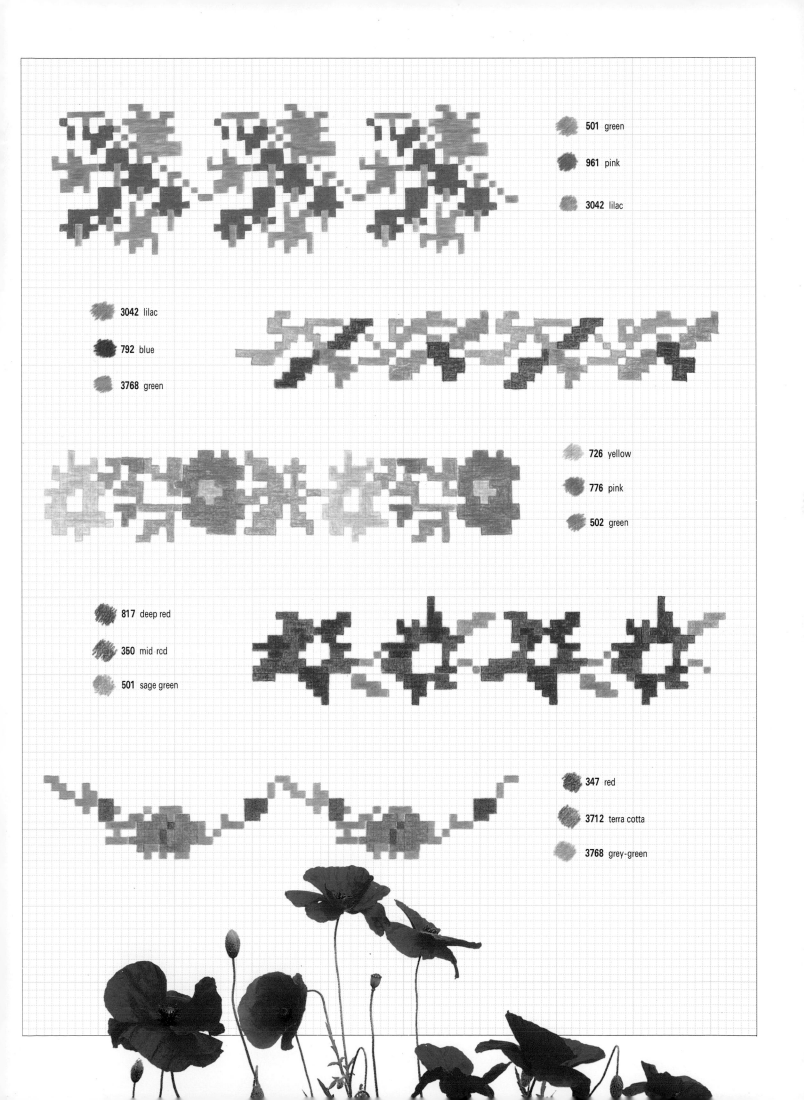

501 green
961 pink
3042 lilac

3042 lilac
792 blue
3768 green

726 yellow
776 pink
502 green

817 deep red
350 mid rcd
501 sage green

347 red
3712 terra cotta
3768 grey-green

CHRISTMAS
Memories

CHRISTMAS WAS ANOTHER EXCITING HOLIDAY.
*Some Christmases we'd go to my aunt's house in
Llanelli. I remember the thrill of seeing the box of
decorations coming down from the top shelf in the
living-room cupboard, and going with my father to
choose the tree in the market. We would decorate it
with tiny white candles, silver tinsel and coloured
glass balls. Finally the fairy with her gauzy white
dress and starred wand would go on top.
On Christmas Eve we'd sit round the fire roasting
chestnuts, and my aunt would tell the story of the
Nativity and tales of her own childhood.
Snow was what I particularly longed for at Christmas.
After a snowfall I'd rush outside to make a snowman.
Sometimes my father would help. We'd make slides by
rubbing our feet over the snow until it turned to ice
and then whizz along it, or toboggan down the slopes
on old tin trays.*

Noël Card

THIS card makes me think of a stained-glass window and the way sunlight on a crisp December day will make the colours glow, lighting up the dim interior of a church.

MATERIALS

DMC stranded embroidery cotton, one skein each of the following colours:

792	*dark blue*
3046	*yellow*
371	*gold*
3072	*grey*
948	*flesh pink*
535	*dark grey*
écru	*cream*
blanc neige	*white*

- Piece of 14-count white or cream Aida cloth, 13 × 13cm (5 × 5in)
- Tapestry needle, size 24
- Greetings card for embroidery, 12 × 9cm (4½ × 3½in), with circular opening 6.5cm (2½in) in diameter (DMC N2501)
- White glue stick

SIZE

The design measures approximately 6.5cm (2½in) in diameter.

TO MAKE THE CARD

Work the design in cross stitch, following the chart and using either two or three strands of thread, as you prefer. Work the outlining and lettering in 535, over the cross stitch, using backstitch and two strands of thread.

Press the completed work. Make up the card following the instructions on page 124.

VARIATION

This design could also be used to make an attractive Christmas tree decoration.

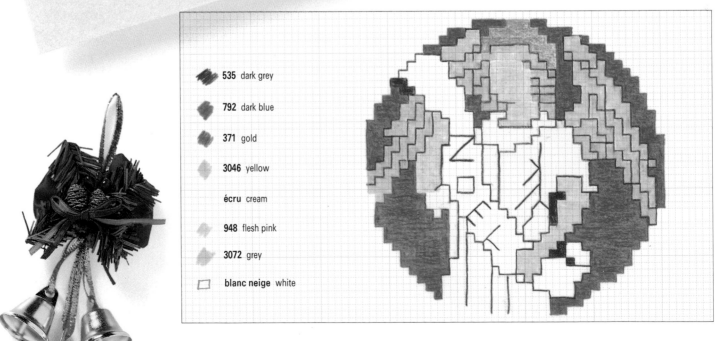

535	dark grey
792	dark blue
371	gold
3046	yellow
écru	cream
948	flesh pink
3072	grey
blanc neige	white

Girl with Holly Greetings Card

This Christmas greeting can be removed from its card and framed as a permanent keepsake.

MATERIALS

DMC stranded embroidery cotton, one skein each of the following colours:

347	red
501	green
793	blue
726	yellow
543	flesh pink
844	dark grey
blanc neige	white

- Piece of 18-count white Aida cloth, 20 × 15cm (8 × 6in)
- Tapestry needle, size 26

- Greetings card for embroidery, 16 × 11cm (6¼ × 4⅜in), with rectangular opening 11 × 7cm (4⅜ × 2¾in) (DMC N2505)
- White glue stick

SIZE

The design measures 4.5 × 10.5cm (1¾ × 4in).

TO MAKE THE CARD

Work the design in cross stitch, following the chart and using one strand of thread. Each square represents one stitch.

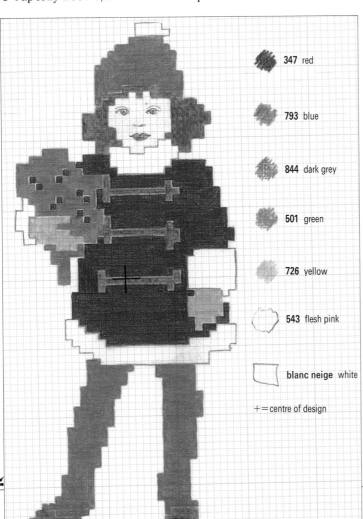

	347	red
	793	blue
	844	dark grey
	501	green
	726	yellow
	543	flesh pink
	blanc neige	white
+	= centre of design	

Press the completed work. Insert it in the card following the instructions on page 124.

VARIATION

This design could also be worked on canvas, using either tent stitch or cross stitch, and framed as a picture. Choose white canvas and white thread for the background.

Boy with Snowball Greetings Card

In the crisp winter air, with snowflakes still drifting down, it's fun to make an *enormous* snowball – and then perhaps a snowman.

MATERIALS
DMC stranded embroidery cotton, one skein each of the following colours:

415	mid-grey
762	light grey
318	dark grey
930	dark blue
931	light blue
3041	mauve
3042	light mauve
948	flesh pink
839	dark brown
blanc neige	*white*

● Piece of 16-count white Aida cloth, 14 × 14cm ($5\frac{1}{2} \times 5\frac{1}{2}$in)
● Tapestry needle, size 24
● Greetings card for embroidery, 12 × 9cm ($4\frac{1}{2} \times 3\frac{1}{2}$in), with circular

opening 6.5cm ($2\frac{1}{2}$in) in diameter (DMC N2501)
● White glue stick

SIZE
The design measures 6.3 × 6.3cm ($2\frac{1}{2} \times 2\frac{1}{2}$in).

TO MAKE THE CARD
Work the design in cross stitch, following the chart and using two strands of thread. Each square represents one stitch. Add the features in backstitch using 839.

Press the completed work. Insert it in the card following the instructions on page 124.

VARIATION
This design could be enlarged to make a picture.

*C*old and raw
The north wind doth blow
Bleak in the morning early;
All the hills are covered with snow,
And winter's now come fairly.

Winter Has Come, ANON

■	930	dark blue
	931	light blue
	318	dark grey
	415	mid-grey
	762	light grey
	3042	light mauve
	3041	mauve
	839	dark brown
	948	flesh pink
	blanc neige	white

Christmas Stockings Card and Paperweight

It's Christmas Eve and time to hang up stockings for Santa to fill! These excited children can be embroidered as a Christmas card for someone special or as a design for a paperweight.

MATERIALS

DMC stranded embroidery cotton, one skein each of the following colours:

823	*dark blue*
824	*dark kingfisher*
517	*light kingfisher*
340	*blue-violet*
3042	*light violet*
413	*dark grey*
948	*flesh pink*
3731	*pink*
370	*bronze*
blanc neige *white*	

● Piece of 25-count cream evenweave cloth, 10 × 13cm (4 × 5in)
● Tapestry needle, size 26
● Greetings card for embroidery, 12 × 9cm (4½ × 3½in), with a circular opening 6.5cm (2½in) in diameter (DMC N2501)
or
● Fluted glass paperweight, 8.7cm (3½in) in diameter. The paperweight shown is available from DMC (see page 126) and is listed as item N858. Buy the paperweight first. You could also use the square paperweight, 6.2 × 6.2cm (2½ × 2½in), N854.

SIZE

The finished design measures approximately 5 × 5cm (2 × 2in).

TO MAKE THE CARD OR PAPERWEIGHT

Work the design in *petit point* – half cross stitch or tent stitch – using two strands of thread and following the chart. One square represents one stitch worked over one thread intersection. For the straight lines use backstitch.

Press the completed work. Mount the card following the instructions on page 124. For the paperweight, also see instructions on page 124.

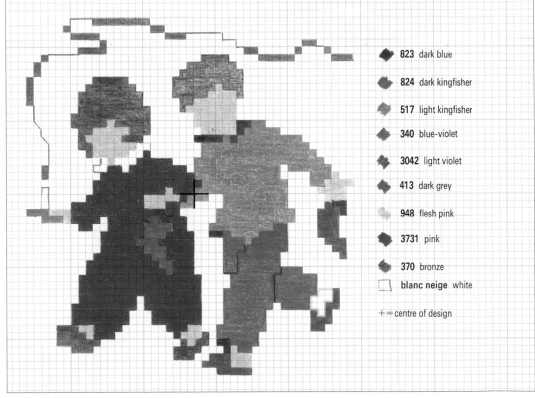

◆	**823**	dark blue
◆	**824**	dark kingfisher
◆	**517**	light kingfisher
◆	**340**	blue-violet
◆	**3042**	light violet
◆	**413**	dark grey
◆	**948**	flesh pink
◆	**3731**	pink
◆	**370**	bronze
☐	**blanc neige**	white

+ = centre of design

Angel with Wreath Card and Paperweight

The Christmas wreath borne by this angel symbolizes the life that continues even in the depths of winter.

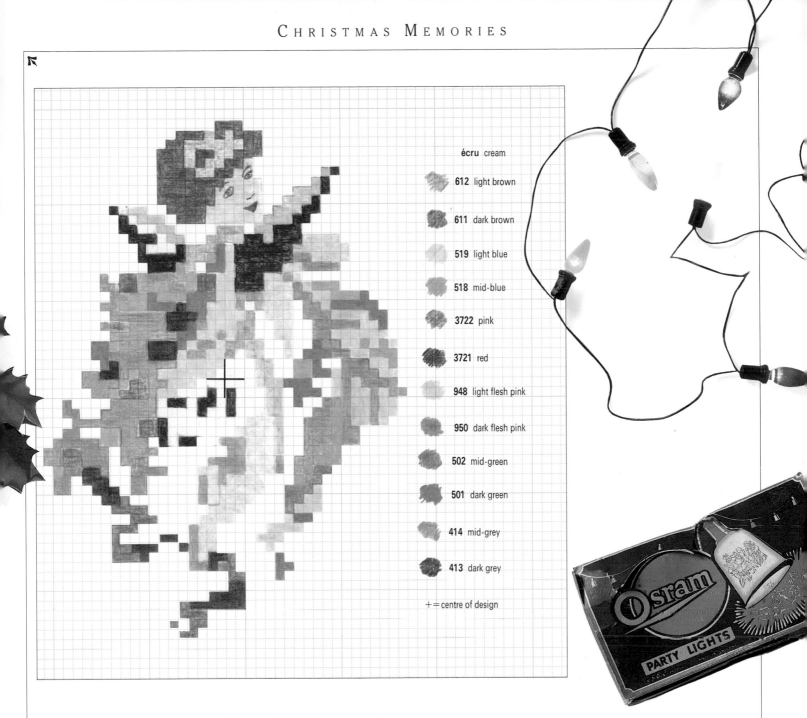

écru cream

612 light brown

611 dark brown

519 light blue

518 mid-blue

3722 pink

3721 red

948 light flesh pink

950 dark flesh pink

502 mid-green

501 dark green

414 mid-grey

413 dark grey

+ = centre of design

MATERIALS

DMC stranded embroidery cotton, one skein each of the following colours:

écru	cream
612	light brown
611	dark brown
519	light blue
518	mid-blue
3722	pink
3721	red
948	light flesh pink
950	dark flesh pink
502	mid-green
501	dark green
414	mid-grey
413	dark grey

● Piece of 18-count white Aida cloth, 13 × 10cm (5 × 4in)
● Tapestry needle, size 26
● Greetings card for embroidery, 12 × 9cm (4½ × 3½in), with rectangular opening measuring 8 × 5.5cm (3⅛ × 2¼in) (DMC N2502) *or*
● Round glass paperweight, 8.7cm (3½in) in diameter. The paperweight shown is

available from DMC (see page 126) and is listed as item N857. Buy the paperweight first; if you cannot obtain one of this size, you will need to adjust the size of the embroidery.

SIZE

The design measures 7 × 5cm (2¾ × 2in).

TO MAKE THE CARD OR PAPERWEIGHT

Work the design in cross stitch, following the chart

and using two strands of thread. Each square represents one stitch.

Press the completed work. Make up the card following the instructions on page 124. For the paperweight, also see instructions on page 124.

VARIATIONS

This design could be made up as a Christmas tree decoration or sewn on a Christmas napkin. It could also be worked on 14- or 16-count Aida to make it larger.

Two Angel Pictures

These two little angels in their golden frames will glow serenely in candlelight.

Larger Angel
MATERIALS
DMC stranded embroidery cotton, one skein each of the following colours:

712	cream
3770	pale flesh pink
3774	deep flesh pink
225	pink
928	pale blue
676	deep yellow
3046	mid-yellow
3047	very pale yellow
612	very light brown
950	deepest flesh pink
453	pinkish grey
3024	grey

C hill December brings the sleet,
Blazing fire and Christmas treat.

The Months, SARA COLERIDGE

- Scraps of 224 (deep pink), 611 (light brown) and 317 (dark grey)
- Piece of 16-count deep cream Aida cloth, 20 × 20cm (8 × 8in)
- Tapestry needle, size 24
- Piece of card, 9 × 10cm (3½ × 4in)
- Strong thread

SIZE
The picture measures 9 × 10cm (3½ × 4in).

TO MAKE THE PICTURE
Work the design in cross stitch, following the chart and using two strands of thread. Each square represents one stitch.

Add the features in backstitch and satin stitch (see page 118), using one strand of 612 for the eyebrows and one strand of 611 for the eyelids. Use 928 for the irises, 317 for the pupils and 224 for the lips.

Press the completed work. Mount it over the card (see page 121) and place it in a frame.

Smaller Angel
MATERIALS
DMC stranded embroidery cotton, one skein each of the following colours:

3024 *grey*	
676 *yellow*	
3770 *pale flesh pink*	
3774 *deep flesh pink*	
612 *brown*	
3047 *very pale yellow*	
3046 *mid-yellow*	
928 *pale blue*	
712 *cream*	

- Scrap of 224 (deep pink)
- Piece of 27-count cream evenweave, 14 × 14cm (5½ × 5½in)
- Tapestry needle, size 26
- Piece of card, 5 × 5cm (2 × 2in)
- Strong thread

SIZE
The picture measures 5 × 5cm (2 × 2in).

TO MAKE THE PICTURE
Work the design in tent stitch or half cross stitch, following the chart and using two strands of thread. Each square represents one stitch worked over one fabric thread intersection. Add the features, in backstitch and satin stitch (see page 118), using one strand of 612 for eyelids, eyebrows and eyes and two strands of 224 for the lips.

Press the completed work. Mount it over the card (see page 121) and place it in a frame.

VARIATIONS
These two pictures could be made the same size, simply by working them on the same count. I made the smaller one to fit a special tiny frame, but it could equally well be worked in cross stitch on 16-count Aida, like the other one. The designs could also be made into tree decorations or embroidered on napkins.

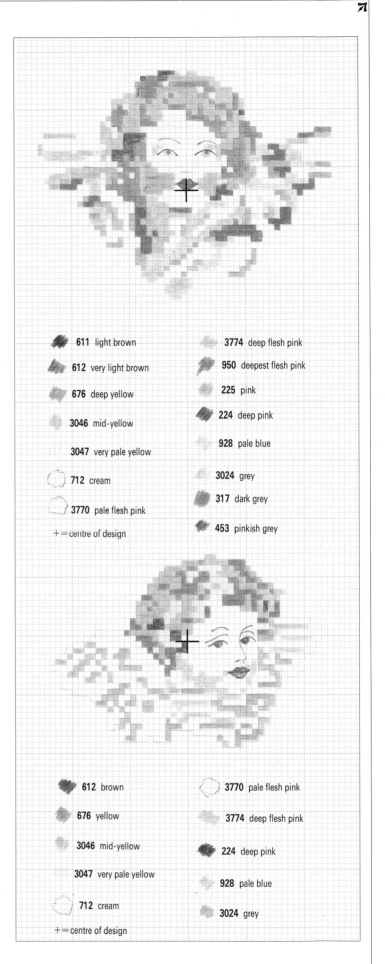

611 light brown
612 very light brown
676 deep yellow
3046 mid-yellow
3047 very pale yellow
712 cream
3770 pale flesh pink
+ = centre of design

3774 deep flesh pink
950 deepest flesh pink
225 pink
224 deep pink
928 pale blue
3024 grey
317 dark grey
453 pinkish grey

612 brown
676 yellow
3046 mid-yellow
3047 very pale yellow
712 cream
+ = centre of design

3770 pale flesh pink
3774 deep flesh pink
224 deep pink
928 pale blue
3024 grey

Girl with Snowball Tree Decoration

Beware! That friendly wave may be followed by a snowball! But it's all part of the wintertime fun.

SIZE
The decoration measures 9 × 5cm (3½ × 2in).

TO MAKE THE DECORATION
Work the design in cross stitch, following the chart and using two strands of thread. Each square represents one stitch. Add the features in backstitch, using 340 for the eyes, 443 for the eyelids, eyebrows and nose, and 315 for the mouth.

Press the completed work. Make up the decoration following the instructions on page 124.

MATERIALS
DMC stranded embroidery cotton, one skein each of the following colours:

792	mid-blue
340	light blue
315	maroon
415	grey
543	flesh pink
311	dark blue
443	brown
blanc neige	white

● Piece of 18-count white Aida cloth, 17 × 13cm (6½ × 5in)
● Tapestry needle, size 26
● Piece of felt, approximately 10 × 6cm (4 × 2½in)
● 38cm (15in) narrow braid
● Piece of 2.5cm (1in)-thick wadding, 9 × 15cm (3½ × 6in), folded in thirds widthwise
● 30cm (12in) of narrow braid
● Small piece of tracing paper

792	mid-blue	543	flesh pink
340	light blue	311	dark blue
315	maroon	443	brown
415	grey	blanc neige	white

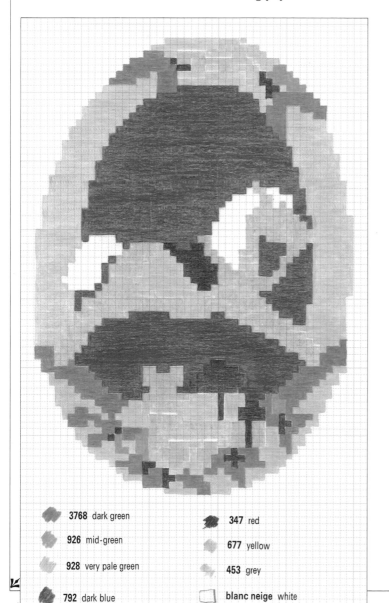

Rocking Horse Tree Decoration

A rocking horse is a present to delight any child, and in a small way this tree decoration recalls the excitement of discovering one beside the tree on Christmas morning.

MATERIALS

DMC stranded embroidery cotton, one skein each of the following colours:

792	dark blue
3768	dark green
453	grey
928	very pale green
347	red
926	mid-green
677	yellow
blanc neige white	

- Piece of 18-count white Aida cloth, 18 × 14cm (7 × 5½in)
- Tapestry needle, size 26
- Piece of felt, 6.5 × 9.5cm (2½ × 3¾in)
- 40cm (16in) of narrow braid
- Piece of 2.5cm (1in)-thick wadding, 12.75 × 9.5cm (5 × 3¾in), folded in half
- Tracing paper

3768 dark green		347 red	
926 mid-green		677 yellow	
928 very pale green		453 grey	
792 dark blue		blanc neige white	

SIZE

The decoration measures 6.5 × 9.5cm (2½ × 3¾in).

TO MAKE THE DECORATION

Work the design in cross stitch, following the chart and using two strands of thread. Each square represents one stitch.

Press the completed work. Make up the decoration following the instructions on page 124.

Pensive Angel Tree Decoration

Perhaps this angel is dreaming of a white Christmas. Whatever the reason for the pensive expression, this tree ornament will introduce a tranquil note into the Christmas festivities.

MATERIALS

DMC stranded embroidery cotton, one skein each of the following colours:

747	*blue*
224	*pink*
869	*light brown*
898	*dark brown*
blanc neige	*white*
762	*grey*
948	*flesh pink*
950	*dark flesh pink*

- Piece of 18-count white or cream Aida cloth, 15 × 12cm (6 × 5in)
- Tapestry needle, size 26
- 40cm (16in) of narrow braid
- Piece of felt, 11 × 8cm (4¼ × 3¼in)
- Piece of 2.5cm (1in)-thick polyester wadding, 9 × 19cm (3½ × 7½in), folded in thirds
- Small piece of tracing paper

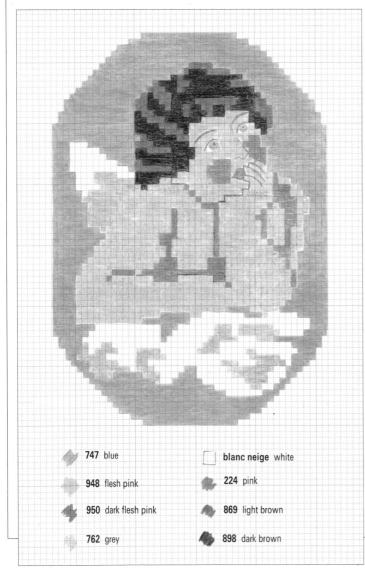

747	blue		blanc neige	white
948	flesh pink		224	pink
950	dark flesh pink		869	light brown
762	grey		898	dark brown

SIZE

The decoration measures 9 × 6.5cm (3½ × 2½in).

TO MAKE THE DECORATION

Work the design in cross stitch, following the chart and using two strands of thread. Each square represents one stitch. Add the features in backstitch and satin stitch (see page 118), using 747 for the eyes, 869 for nose, eyelids, pupils and eyebrows, and 224 for the mouth.

Press the completed work. Make up the decoration following the instructions on page 124.

VARIATIONS

This design could be worked on 14-count Aida to make a picture, or embroidered on to a Christmas napkin.

Golden-Haired Angel Tree Decoration

Gazing out of a deep blue sky, this golden-haired angel brings a message of peace and good will.

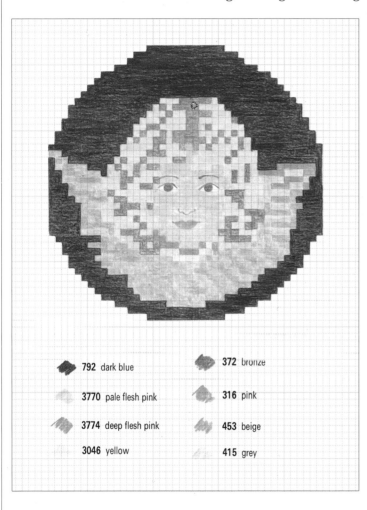

	792	dark blue		372	bronze
	3770	pale flesh pink		316	pink
	3774	deep flesh pink		453	beige
	3046	yellow		415	grey

- 40cm (16in) of narrow braid
- Small piece of tracing paper

SIZE

The decoration measures 6.5cm (2½in) in diameter.

TO MAKE THE DECORATION

Work the design in cross stitch, following the chart and using two strands of thread. Each square

represents one stitch. Add the features in backstitch and satin stitch (see page 118), using 792 for the eyes, 372 for the nose, eyelids and eyebrows, and 316 for the mouth.

Press the completed work. Make up the decoration following the instructions on page 124.

VARIATIONS

This design could be used for a greetings card or a paperweight, or embroidered on a napkin.

MATERIALS

DMC stranded embroidery cotton, one skein each of the following colours:

792	*dark blue*
3770	*pale flesh pink*
3774	*deep flesh pink*
453	*beige*
415	*grey*
3046	*yellow*
372	*bronze*

- Scrap of 316 (pink)
- Piece of 16-count white or cream Aida cloth, 10 × 10cm (4 × 4in)
- Tapestry needle, size 24
- Piece of felt, 7 × 7cm (3 × 3in)
- Piece of 2.5cm (1in)-thick wadding, 6.5 × 19.5cm (2½ × 8in), folded in thirds widthwise and cut into a circle to fit

Christmas Tree Pincushion

Why not make a few of these little scented pincushions to have handy when someone unexpectedly gives you a Christmas present?

positioning the top line six fabric threads from the fold. Fill in with cross stitch. You can use either two or three strands of thread. Each square of the chart represents one stitch worked over *three* threads of the fabric.

Press the completed work, and make up the pincushion following the instructions on page 121.

MATERIALS

DMC stranded embroidery cotton, one skein of the following colour:

798 *dark blue*

● Piece of 28-count *eau-de-nil* evenweave cloth, 18 × 10.5cm (7 × 4in)
● Tapestry needle, size 26
● Piece of 2.5cm (1in)-thick wadding, 18 × 10.5cm (7 × 4in), plus another piece, 9 × 10.5cm (3½ × 4in)

● Small amount of lavender or pot-pourri

SIZE

The pincushion measures about 8 × 8cm (3 × 3in).

TO MAKE THE PINCUSHION

Fold the material in half across its width so that it measures 9 × 10.5cm (3½ × 4in). Work the design on one half, beginning with the Holbein stitch outline (see page 117) and

798 dark blue

+ = centre of design

Angel Bookmark

Two Christmas angels bearing an evergreen garland
adorn this bookmark, which is quickly worked on
Aida band.

MATERIALS

DMC stranded embroidery
cotton, one skein each of the
following colours:

950	dark flesh pink
948	pale flesh pink
3047	yellow
611	bronze
797	dark blue
501	green
blanc neige	white

● Piece of 5cm (2in)-wide
Aida band, 24cm (9½in) long
● Tapestry needle, size 24
● Piece of thin lining fabric,
7 × 18cm (2¾ × 7in)

SIZE

The bookmark measures
24 × 5cm (9½ × 2in),
including fringe.
Actual design measures
4.5 × 16cm (1¾ × 6¼in).

TO MAKE THE BOOKMARK

Work the design in cross
stitch, following the chart
and using two strands of
thread. Each square of
the chart represents one
stitch.

Press the completed work.
Apply the lining and finish
the ends of the Aida band,
following the instructions on
page 121.

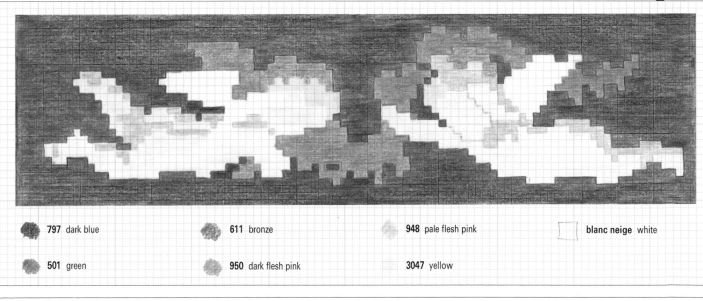

| | 797 dark blue | | 611 bronze | | 948 pale flesh pink | | blanc neige white |
| | 501 green | | 950 dark flesh pink | | 3047 yellow | | |

Snowman Picture

Capture the fun of making a snowman by stitching this jolly picture on snowy white evenweave fabric.

MATERIALS

DMC stranded embroidery cotton in the following colours:

356	*rust red*
813	*light blue*

317	*mid-grey*
840	*mid-brown*
841	*light brown*
3047	*pale yellow*
3041	*lilac*
3740	*deep lilac*
311	*dark blue*

3770	*flesh pink*
3768	*green*
312	*mid-blue*
413	*dark grey*
(one skein each)	
415	*light grey*
(two skeins)	

- Piece of 28-count white evenweave cloth, 30 × 30cm (12 × 12in)
- Tapestry needle, size 26
- Piece of card, 18 × 20cm (7 × 8in)
- Strong thread

SIZE

The picture measures 19 × 21cm (7½ × 8¼in).

TO MAKE THE PICTURE

Work the design in cross stitch, following the chart and using two strands of thread. Each square represents one stitch, worked over two fabric threads. Outline the snowman in backstitch using two strands of 413.

Press the completed work, mount it over the card (see page 121) and place it in a frame.

VARIATION

This design could also be worked in tent stitch on canvas, using tapestry wool and filling in the background with white wool. (See the stranded cotton–tapestry wool colour conversion chart on page 127.)

3047 pale yellow	**841** light brown	**3041** lilac	**312** mid-blue	**3768** green
3770 flesh pink	**840** mid-brown	**3740** deep lilac	**311** dark blue	
415 light grey	**356** rust red	**813** light blue	**3172** mid-grey	

CHART ON PAGES 110–11

Sledging Picture

Snow becomes a magic carpet if you've got a sledge
– especially one that's big enough to share with
some friends.

MATERIALS

DMC tapestry wool (Laine Colbert) in the following colours:

7304	*bright blue*
7295	*slate blue*
7266	*deep mauve*
7262	*light mauve*
7701	*dark green*
7473	*dark yellow*
7451	*flesh pink*
7354	*deep pink*
7194	*light pink*
7292	*dark grey*
(one skein each)	
7905	*pale yellow*
7423	*light brown*
7702	*light green*
(two skeins each)	
7415	*dark brown*
7715	*light grey*
(three skeins each)	
blanc	*white*
(eight skeins)	

● Piece of 10-gauge white single-thread canvas 48 × 64cm (19 × 25in)
● Tapestry needle, size 22
● Piece of card 29 × 44cm (11½ × 17½in)
● Strong thread

SIZE

The picture measures 29 × 44cm (11½ × 17½in).

TO MAKE THE PICTURE

Work the design in tent stitch, following the chart and using one strand of thread. Each square represents one stitch.

Block the completed work (see page 120). Mount it over card (see page 121) and place it in a frame.

VARIATION

This sledging design could also be worked in cross stitch on white evenweave, leaving the snowy background unworked. (See the stranded cotton–tapestry wool colour conversion chart on page 127.)

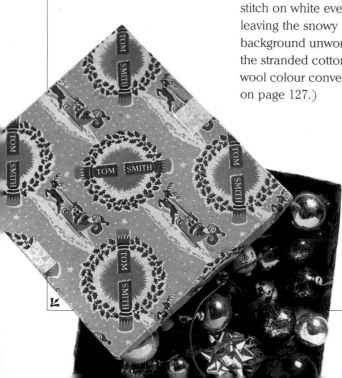

H sst! There's a stirring – there's a wind in the snow;
A whirring of birds on the wing.

Listen, WALTER DE LA MARE

CHART FOR SLEDGING PICTURE

7304 bright blue	**7262** light mauve	**7702** light green
7295 slate blue	**7194** light pink	**7701** dark green
	7354 deep pink	**7423** light brown

7415 dark brown	**7266** deep mauve	blanc white
7715 light grey	**7905** pale yellow	**7451** flesh pink
7292 dark grey	**7473** dark yellow	scrap of dark brown, grey or black

Angel Table Mat

Singing Christmas carols, this angel will strike a joyful note on your Yuletide table linen.

MATERIALS

DMC stranded embroidery cotton, one skein each of the following colours:

453	grey
3046	deep yellow
3047	pale yellow
3041	dark violet
3042	light violet
3774	dark flesh pink
948	pale flesh pink
372	bronze

● Piece of 25-count cream evenweave cloth, 31 × 41cm (12 × 16in) (70cm [27½in] of 140cm [55in]-wide fabric will yield six table mats)
● Tapestry needle, size 26

SIZE

The design measures 18 × 7.5cm (7 × 3in).

TO MAKE THE TABLE MAT

First mark the position for the angel on the fabric with a few tacking stitches. Mark the right-hand edge of the design 2cm (¾in) from the raw edge of the fabric; mark the top and bottom edges 6.5cm (2½in) from the upper and lower edges. Finally, count 20 squares in from the marked right-hand edge of the design and 45 squares down from the top marked edge, and mark the centre of the design (see page 118). Begin stitching here.

Work the design in cross stitch, following the chart and using two strands of thread. Each square represents one stitch worked over two fabric threads.

Press the completed work. Pull out one fabric thread 1.2cm (½in) in from all four edges. Work a line of zigzag stitch, or oversew by hand along this inner edge, in cream thread. Remove the outer fabric threads to form a fringe.

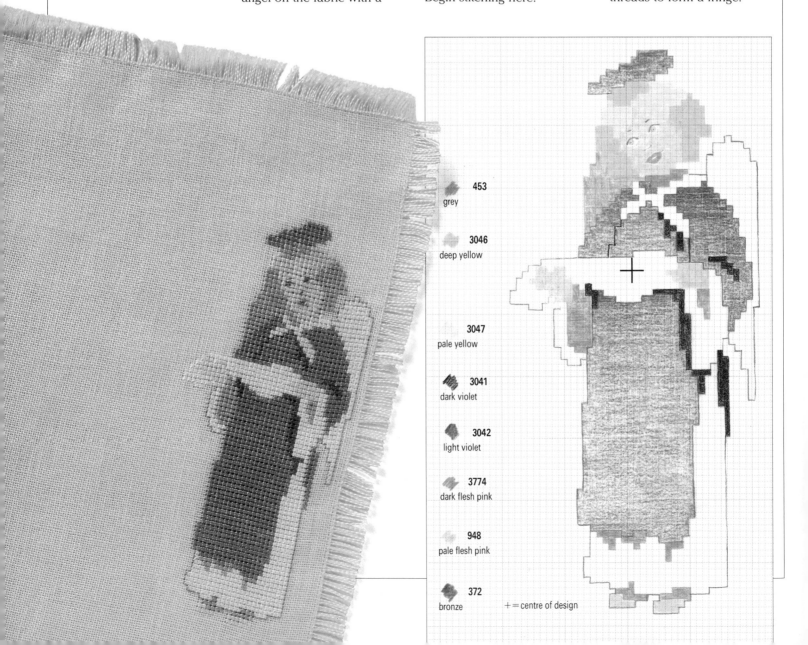

453 grey

3046 deep yellow

3047 pale yellow

3041 dark violet

3042 light violet

3774 dark flesh pink

948 pale flesh pink

372 bronze   += centre of design

Yule Log Paperweight

The old English tradition of bringing in the Yule Log makes a lively design for a paperweight – perhaps to put on top of all those Christmas bills!

MATERIALS

DMC stranded embroidery cotton, one skein each of the following colours:

501	green
347	red
311	blue
725	yellow
316	pink
948	flesh pink
3042	lilac
839	dark brown
840	light brown
333	purple

● Piece of 18-count cream Aida cloth, 13 × 13cm (5 × 5in)
● Tapestry needle, size 26
● Round glass paperweight, 8.8cm (3½in). The paperweight shown is available from DMC (see page 126) and is listed as item N857. Buy the paperweight first; if you cannot obtain one of this size, you will need to adjust the size of the embroidery accordingly.

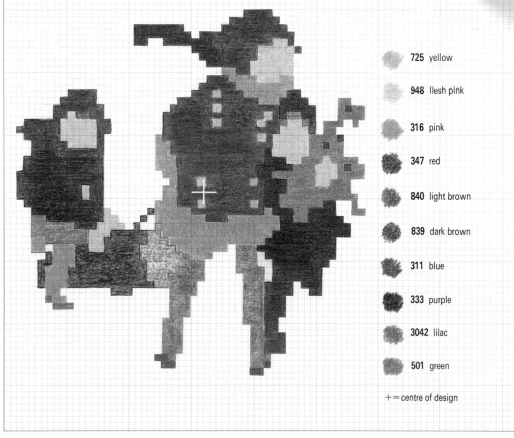

725 yellow

948 flesh pink

316 pink

347 red

840 light brown

839 dark brown

311 blue

333 purple

3042 lilac

501 green

+ = centre of design

SIZE

The finished design measures 6.5 × 7cm (2½ × 2¾in).

TO MAKE THE PAPERWEIGHT

Work the design in cross stitch, following the chart and using two strands of thread. Each square represents one stitch.

Press the completed work. Make up the paperweight following the instructions on page 124.

VARIATIONS

This design could equally well be used for a Christmas card or a tree decoration, worked on finer count fabric.

Basic Techniques

I n the following pages you will find instructions for all the techniques required for the projects in this book, as well as useful information on choosing and handling materials. Once you become familiar with these techniques and materials, you will be able to vary the projects if you like, to suit your own taste. You may wish, for example, to work one of the cross stitch designs on needlepoint canvas, or simply to change the scale of the work. Most of the projects include one or more suggested variations, but you may think of others.

Materials

EVENWEAVE To form the perfect square needed for cross stitch, you must use an evenweave fabric. This kind of fabric has the same number of warp (vertical) and weft (horizontal) threads over a given measurement. This number is called the fabric's 'count'. A 22-count fabric has 22 threads to 2.5cm (1in).

The easiest fabric for beginners to use is Aida cloth. This is woven with groups of threads – normally four. The intersection of four warp and four weft threads makes a little square, over which each stitch is worked. The four tiny holes around each square are easy to see and to stitch into.

Aida cloth is available from 6-count (the binca of primary school days!) to 18-count, and comes in a good variety of colours.

There is also an easy-count Aida, which is woven with a removable grid of contrasting threads every 10 squares. This makes it easier to count fabric squares and is very useful where the chart used for the design is divided into 10-square units – as are most of the charts in this book – or where you are

positioning lettering and other elements in a sampler, for example. The grid threads pull out easily after the stitching is complete. Easy-count Aida is more expensive than the plain kind and comes in fewer sizes, and only in white or cream, but you may find it worth using for some complex designs.

Another kind of evenweave is Hardanger, which is used for the traditional Norwegian embroidery of that name and for other kinds of counted thread work, including cross stitch. It is woven with pairs of threads, 22 to 2.5cm (1in), and comes in a good range of colours.

Single-thread evenweave – in which single warp and weft threads cross each other – includes a great variety of fabrics, both natural and synthetic, ranging from coarse to fine, some with as many as 36 threads to 2.5cm (1in). On single-thread evenweave, cross stitches are worked over two threads (or more) in each direction. Thus a 36-count single-thread evenweave has the same count as an 18-count Aida.

CANVAS There are three different kinds of needlepoint canvas: double-thread, or Penelope; single-thread, or mono;

and interlock. This last type resembles single-thread canvas, but the vertical threads are actually two fine threads, which are tightly twisted together so that they 'lock' at the intersections. This is intended to prevent the canvas threads from being pulled out of alignment during the stitching. However, if you are not using a frame, even interlock may warp somewhat, and you may prefer to use ordinary single-thread canvas, which will better withstand the greater tension exerted on a badly warped stitched canvas during the blocking process.

Penelope canvas is useful for projects in which you wish to work some areas in finer stitches than elsewhere (such as the seagulls on pages 34–5): the paired threads can be separated with the needle, allowing you to stitch over the individual threads.

All three types of canvas are graded according to the number of mesh per 2.5cm (1in) – mesh being the intersection of the threads. You will also find it described in terms of threads or holes to the inch. Yet another designation is 'gauge'. All of these terms mean the same thing: a 12-mesh or 12-gauge canvas has 12

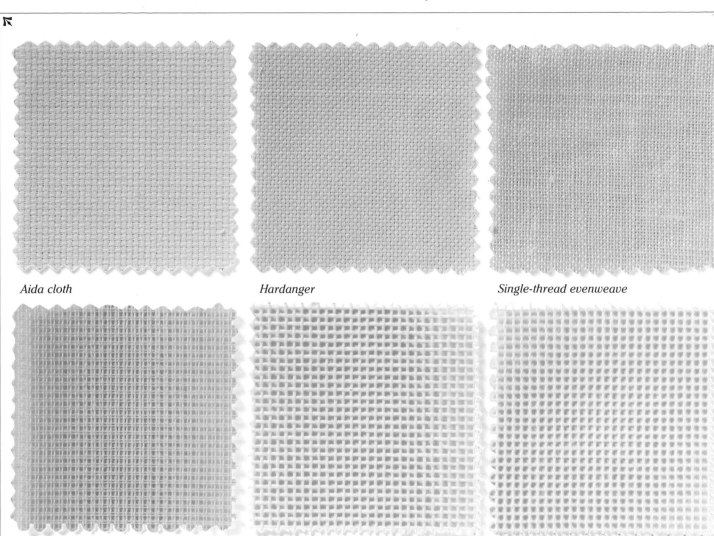

Aida cloth

Hardanger

Single-thread evenweave

Double-thread or Penelope canvas

Single-thread or mono canvas

Interlock canvas

threads/holes to the inch. Penelope tends to be referred to in terms of holes, since it actually has twice as many threads to the inch as an equivalent mono canvas.

Canvas comes in a wide range of mesh sizes – from 3- or 5-mesh rug canvas to 28-mesh. You can enlarge or reduce the size of a design simply by choosing a coarser or finer canvas than that specified. It also comes in several colours, including shades of beige, yellow, and white. Although the canvas should be well covered by the stitching, its colours may show through very slightly, and so the choice of canvas colour depends on the overall colouring of the design. A design that features light colours is normally best worked on white canvas, whereas for dark colours a beige background is preferable. A white interlock canvas

has been used for most of the needlepoint projects in this book.

THREADS

The threads used for the projects in this book are DMC stranded embroidery cotton and DMC tapestry wool (Laine Colbert). Each comes in well over 350 colours.

The stranded cotton (also called embroidery floss) consists of six fine threads, which can easily be separated to achieve the required thickness. It is mercerized, which gives it a silky texture, and colourfast, and comes in 8m (8¾yd) skeins. Stranded cotton should be used in lengths of no more than 45cm (18in) to prevent fraying.

Tapestry wool, too, comes in 8m (8¾yd) skeins. It is used in a single thickness and in lengths of no more than about 60cm (23in) to prevent the

wool from becoming frayed as it passes through the canvas. Make sure you retain the wool's normal twist, to prevent tangling and thinning. Occasionally allowing the needle to hang free will help with this.

NEEDLES

A tapestry needle should be used for all cross stitch and needlepoint (except for cross stitch worked over a canvas grid, as described on page 117). This kind of needle has a blunt point, which slips between the fabric or canvas threads without snagging. Choose a needle that can easily be threaded with the required wool or cotton and that will pass through the fabric without tugging.

Needle sizes are specified in the projects, but here is a rough guide for working your own adaptations or original projects: 10-, 11-count (or mesh size), size 22 needle; 14-, 16-count, size 24; 18-, 22- and 25-count, size 26. A larger needle size can be used if you prefer.

Stitches

The main stitches used in this book are tent stitch and cross stitch. Half cross is used for a few projects, and various other stitches are used for details and in making up some items.

CROSS STITCH Cross stitch consists of two diagonal stitches, one on top of the other, worked over two or more fabric threads or over a single intersection of Aida cloth or Penelope canvas. It can be worked in horizontal or vertical rows, or diagonally. For horizontal rows, work all the bottom stitches first,

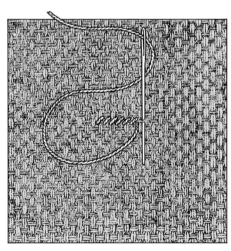

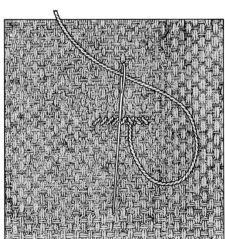

Horizontal cross stitch

then work back over these to complete the stitch. If you prefer, you can have all the bottom stitches slanting from lower right to top left and the top stitches from lower left to top right; but you must be consistent.

When working the stitch vertically or diagonally, complete each stitch before moving on to the next one.

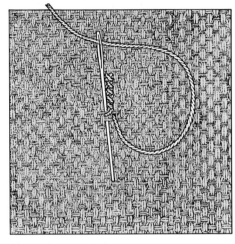

Vertical cross stitch

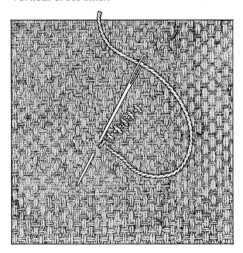

Diagonal cross stitch

TENT STITCH This is the smallest of all needlepoint stitches, covering only one mesh of the canvas on the right side. There are two versions of the stitch, continental and basketweave, or diagonal.

Continental tent is worked in horizontal or vertical rows. The needle is taken under two vertical threads and one horizontal one for each stitch. When one row has been worked, turn the canvas and come back.

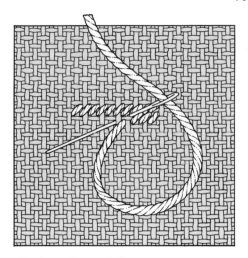

Continental tent stitch

The simplicity of this method makes it well suited to patterned areas, but it tends to pull the work out of shape.

The slightly more complex basketweave tent can be used for larger areas of one colour; it produces less distortion of the canvas. This version is stitched from upper left to lower right (having begun at the top right corner), and then back up again. On the downward journey the needle moves vertically, and on the upward row, horizontally. (Note that in all stitch diagrams the needle is shown as if flat, whereas if you are using a frame it will be perpendicular to the surface.) On the wrong side the stitches are horizontal and vertical, forming a basketweave pattern (hence the name), which keeps the mesh reasonably in true.

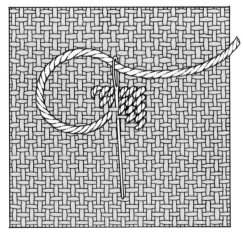

Basketweave tent stitch

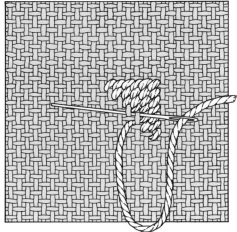

Basketweave tent stitch

Although tent stitch is normally worked on canvas, I have used it on evenweave for some of these projects – combining the fine detail of this stitch with the more pliable quality of evenweave.

HALF CROSS STITCH Although it looks like tent stitch, half cross does not cover the canvas so well, and the resulting article is not as hard-wearing. The needle goes over one mesh each time, but under only one horizontal thread. This stitch is more economical of thread than true tent stitch: an 8m (8¾yd) skein of tapestry wool covers 65 sq cm (10sq in) in half cross stitch, but only 31.5sq cm (5sq in) in tent stitch.

Half cross stitch

I have used half cross stitch for a couple of the small projects worked on evenweave, because it is less bulky on the wrong side than tent stitch.

CROSS STITCH OVER A CANVAS GRID If you wish to work a cross stitch design on a non-evenweave fabric, or directly on to a garment or pillowcase, for example, you can do so by working it over canvas. Any needlepoint canvas will do for this – so long as it is not interlock – but you can buy a special waste canvas, which has every fifth horizontal thread coloured, for easy counting. It is double-thread, which is somewhat easier to stitch over than single-thread, and it comes in mesh sizes ranging from 8 to 14.

First cut a piece of waste canvas slightly larger than the motif to be stitched, and tack [baste] it to the fabric, taking care to align the canvas threads with the weave of the fabric. Work the cross stitch through both canvas and fabric. When the embroidery is complete, moisten the canvas, then carefully pull out the canvas threads, one by one. Rinse the item thoroughly to remove any canvas dressing from the fabric.

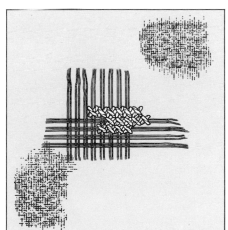

Cross stitch over a canvas grid

BLANKET STITCH Also called buttonhole stitch, this is often used to finish an edge or join two turned-under edges decoratively, as for the Assisi work pincushions. For the pincushions, space the stitches as in the diagram, two fabric threads apart and crossing three fabric threads.

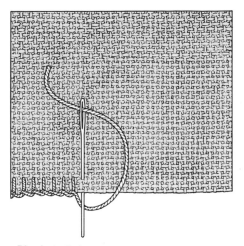

Blanket stitch

HOLBEIN STITCH This stitch is also known as double running stitch. It consists of two lines of even running stitches, each filling the spaces left by the other, so as to produce a solid line. The effect is the same on both sides of the fabric. It is often used to outline Assisi work motifs, which are left blank

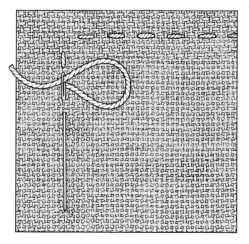

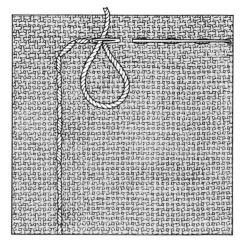

Holbein stitch

and surrounded by a solid cross-stitched background. The running stitches can cover any number of threads, so long as it is the same number throughout.

Work the first line of running stitch around all the outlines. Then work back in the opposite direction, filling in the spaces left on the first journey.

BACKSTITCH This stitch is often used to produce a fine line, such as eyebrows. You may prefer to use a crewel needle, which has a sharp point, to work very small backstitches.

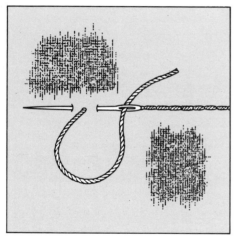

Backstitch

SATIN STITCH I have used this stitch for certain facial features, such as lips and the iris of the eye. Begin at the centre of a shape to establish the slant, then work out to either end, keeping the stitches parallel and close to each other.

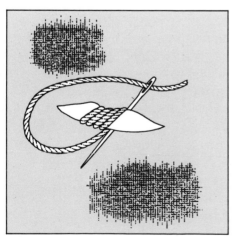

Satin stitch

OVERSEWING This stitch is used to prevent a raw edge from fraying (machine zigzag can be used instead).

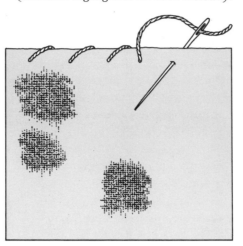

Oversewing

SLIPSTITCH This stitch is often used to join two turned-under edges, as on the gap left in a cushion cover. Use a sewing needle and (usually) a single strand of sewing thread.

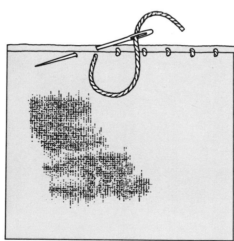

Slipstitch

Preparing Fabrics

When cutting fabric or canvas for a project, make sure to allow ample margins around the design area. A margin of 7 or 8cm (3in) is adequate for the smaller cross stitch projects; but leave 10cm (4in) for the larger needlepoint projects. Margins are included in the design instructions.

To prevent the edges from fraying, you can work machine zigzag stitch or

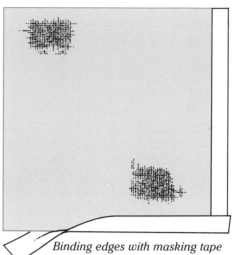

Binding edges with masking tape

oversewing around the edges, or you can bind them with masking tape.

For those projects worked on evenweave, with part of the fabric exposed (those whose charts have a + in the centre), you must mark the vertical and horizontal centres of the fabric so that you can position the design correctly. Fold the fabric in half lengthwise and widthwise, lightly crease the folds and tack [baste] along the creases. The intersection of the threads is the centre of the fabric. Alternatively, you can mark along the creases with a water-soluble pen (test this on spare fabric first). Do not use an ordinary pencil, because it will rub off on to the threads and be difficult to remove.

For all-over designs, draw the outline on the fabric, counting off the same number of canvas or fabric threads as there are squares on the chart (multiply this number by the number of threads covered by each stitch, if appropriate). If you start in one corner, you can simply mark that corner, begin stitching there and work outward, following the chart.

Using a Frame

Some people prefer to work cross stitch in the hand. Aida cloth is heavily sized, so it should retain its shape, if you stitch with an even tension, as cross stitch pulls the work in opposite directions all the time. However, I find it much easier to use a frame, which also gives me much better results, for both cross stitch and needlepoint.

Continental tent stitch, in particular, pulls the work diagonally in the same direction all the time, and if the work is not framed it can end up looking like a parallelogram, rather than a rectangle. The 'scooping' method of stitching, used when the material is hand-held, assists in this distortion of the canvas, whereas with a frame you must 'stab' the stitches vertically, which exerts less strain on the canvas threads. (Keeping one hand above the frame and one below speeds up the stitching process.) I also find that stitches made using this technique are more even than those made by scooping.

RING FRAMES Also known as hoops, these come in many different sizes, and some are made to fit on to a table or floor stand or clamp on to a chair arm, which leaves both hands free for stitching. They are suitable for evenweave but not for canvas, which is too stiff to fit between the rings.

To mount fabric in a ring frame, adjust the screw on the outer frame so that this ring fits smoothly, but not tightly, over the inner one. Separate the rings, place the fabric over the inner ring on a smooth, hard surface, and press the outer ring down over it. The fabric should be quite taut; if it is not,

remove the ring and tighten the screw slightly. Tightening the screw after inserting the fabric will prevent it from slipping but will not make the surface more taut. If you are right-handed, place the screw at the upper left part of the frame; if left-handed, at the upper right – to prevent the thread from getting caught while you are stitching.

When you have finished work for the day, remove the fabric from the hoop to release the pressure on the stitches caught between the rings. Re-position the hoop slightly the next day to avoid leaving marks on the fabric. Oil from the skin can easily build up on the fabric round the edges of the hoop, so always wash your hands before starting work. If the project is a large one, taking a long time, it is a good idea to roll the work up in tissue or a clean white cloth when you are not working on it.

STRETCHER FRAMES These rectangular frames are made from inexpensive wooden stretchers, available from art shops in many different sizes. The mitred ends slot together. To attach the fabric or canvas, mark the centre of each stretcher and the centre of each edge of the fabric and fasten the fabric at these points, using drawing pins and pulling it taut. Then work outward to the corners, inserting the drawing pins at 1.5–2cm ($\frac{1}{2}$–$\frac{3}{4}$in) intervals and working on alternate sides.

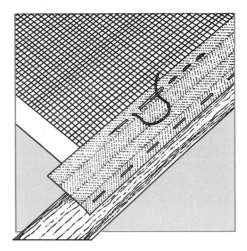

Mounting fabric on a slate frame

SLATE FRAMES Also known as scroll, roller or square frames, these are ideal for large needlepoint projects, as they expose a large area of canvas, while allowing part of the canvas to be rolled up at top and/or bottom, if desired. The maximum width of canvas that the frames will accommodate is determined by the length of the webbing on the top and bottom rollers. Slate frames come in a good range of sizes, and some are equipped with table or floor stands for greater ease in stitching. The simplest of these are fastened with wing nuts. In the more expensive models favoured by professional embroiderers, the side battens are fixed in place with knobs or pegs, and the sides of the fabric are laced to these battens with string, producing a very taut surface.

To mount canvas or other fabric in a slate frame, first mark the centre point of the webbing strips. Also mark the centre of the upper and lower edges of the canvas. Fasten these points to the webbing with a few stitches, then work backstitch out to one side, then the other, taking care to align one canvas thread with the edge of the webbing and fastening off securely. Roll any excess canvas around the top or bottom rollers, then place it into the wooden side sections. Keeping the canvas as taut as possible, tighten the wing nuts at both sides, top and bottom.

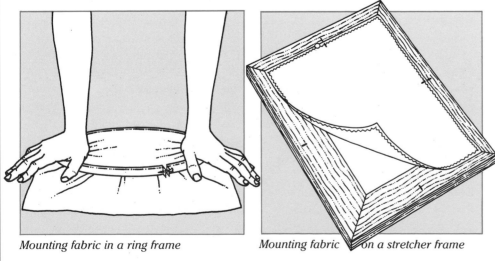

Mounting fabric in a ring frame   *Mounting fabric on a stretcher frame*

OTHER EQUIPMENT

You will need two pairs of scissors: a very sharp-pointed pair for cutting threads and some dressmaker's shears for cutting fabric and canvas.

A thread organizer, which includes a thread-measuring card, a thread list and a project card, is a useful, though not essential, accessory.

A magnetic board will hold a chart at an easy angle for reading; the magnets help you find your place in the chart. Another useful accessory is a line magnifier.

A stitch converter will be useful if you want to change the scale of a project.

FOLLOWING A CHART

The charts in this book all follow the same style: each square on the grid represents a single stitch – or the equivalent space on the fabric or canvas. If the stitches are worked over a single intersection of Aida cloth, then a single square will correspond to one of these intersections; if they are worked over two fabric threads in each direction, then a blank square will correspond to two fabric threads. Every 10th line on the chart is generally heavier than the others. This will help you to count the stitches and spaces.

Designs worked on evenweave that is left partly exposed include a cross + at the centre of the design. Begin stitching at this point and work outward.

The key given with each chart identifies the exact thread colours to be used throughout the design (note that the photographs represent the colours more accurately than the charts).

STITCHING TIPS

When beginning a new thread, run it under the stitches on the wrong side, fastening it with a backstitch; or knot the thread, take it from front to back, and work over it; then cut off the knot.

Do not use a knot on the back of the work, as it may leave a visible bump or pull through. To fasten the end, run the needle under about five stitches and cut the thread carefully, close to the work. Do not carry thread from one part of the design to another for more than about 1.5cm ($\frac{1}{2}$in), and wherever possible run the thread under previously worked stitches.

When you are working with several colours at once, temporarily fasten any threads that you are not using on the right side of the fabric, out of the way of the stitching, using a couple of backstitches. You can easily retrieve the thread when it is next needed, and you avoid having a lot of dangling (and tangled) threads underneath.

Never leave a needle in the design area of the fabric, where it may leave a rust stain. If you prick your finger and blood gets on the work, wash it off immediately with cold water.

I find it best to stitch the design first and the background, if any, later. This is a purely personal preference, and some people choose to stitch from the top of the work to the bottom.

WASHING AND PRESSING

If the design has become soiled during the stitching, wash it in cool water and soap flakes, without rubbing the stitched surface. Rinse it thoroughly in cool water, but do not wring. Roll it in a clean, dry towel to absorb excess water. Then unroll it, right side down, on to a clean, dry cloth, such as a folded cotton sheet or towel, and cover it with a pressing cloth – a cotton pillowcase or a white linen tea towel will do. Press with the iron at the cotton setting, until the needlework is dry.

If you have kept the work perfectly clean, you can omit the washing and simply press it, face down, on a well-padded surface, using either a steam iron or a dry iron, set for cotton, over a pressing cloth.

BLOCKING NEEDLEPOINT

Even if you have used a frame, canvas may be pulled out of shape in the course of the stitching, and you will need to pull it back into shape.

For this you will need carpet tacks, a hammer, a clean cloth larger than the canvas (I use an old white cotton pillowcase), a clean board (such as chipboard) and a set square [right-angled triangle]. Pin the cloth to the board. Then thoroughly dampen the back of the needlepoint with water from a plant-misting bottle, and place it face down on the cloth. Line up one edge of the needlepoint with a ruler or the edge of the board, and tack it in place, positioning the tacks at least 2.5cm (1in) away from the edge of the stitching and spacing them about 1.5cm ($\frac{1}{2}$in) apart. Do not hammer them in too hard, as they will almost certainly need to be moved. Using the set square [triangle] to ensure that the corner is at a right angle, pull an adjacent edge into shape and tack it down. Continue around the work, pulling it taut, re-dampening and replacing the tacks where necessary. The blocked work should be flat, with four right-angled corners. It is difficult work, needing strong hands; you can have it done by a specialist framer.

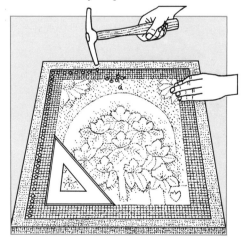

Blocking needlepoint

Leave the work to dry gradually for at least 36 hours. If the work was pulled badly out of shape, it may need to be re-blocked, especially if it is to be made into a cushion. A picture will be stretched and fastened to a board during the framing process, and this, as well as the frame, should keep it square.

Making-up Instructions

MOUNTING A PICTURE OVER CARD

After pressing or blocking the embroidery, place it face down on a flat surface. Lay a piece of card [illustration board] cut to the finished size on top of the work, and pin the fabric to the edges at top and bottom. Check the right side to make sure that the design is straight. Insert more pins along the top and bottom edges. Then, using strong thread – still on the reel – and herringbone stitch, as shown below, lace the two edges together from the centre out to one side. Pull more thread from the reel as required. Fasten off securely.

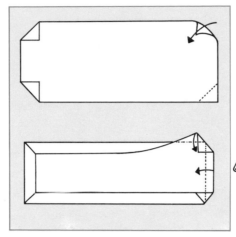

Preparing lining for a bookmark

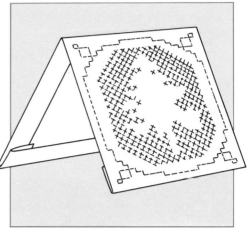

Turning under fabric edges

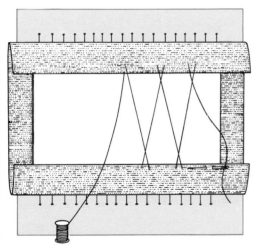

Lacing fabric over card

Cut off the thread, allowing a little more than you used for the previous stitching, re-thread the needle and work herringbone stitch to the other end. Before fastening off, pull all the stitches so that the thread lies fairly taut, without bending the card.

Repeat the same process to lace the opposite sides together, tucking the corners under slightly so that they do not extend past the edges.

FINISHING A BOOKMARK

To finish a bookmark worked on Aida band, you can simply oversew or machine zigzag just above and below the embroidery, then fringe the ends.

Or, if you don't want the wrong side of the embroidery to be visible, you can apply a lining. Choose a lightweight fabric, such as cotton lawn or China silk, which will take a crease well. Fold under the edges as shown, mitring the corners, to make the lining measure the same size as the embroidery, and press. Slipstitch the lining over the wrong side of the work.

ASSISI WORK PINCUSHIONS

After pressing the embroidered fabric flat, turn under the edges all round. First turn under the side edges: count six threads out from each side of the embroidery, and press, taking care to press exactly along the weave. Then count six threads up from the top of the embroidery and press. Then turn under the fabric six threads from the bottom of the embroidery and press again. Finally, turn under and press the lower edge of the back section to make it the same size as the front.

Cut a piece of wadding slightly smaller than the embroidered fabric (opened flat but with edges turned under). Cut another piece of wadding, less than half the size of the first piece, and place it on one end. This will help to give the pincushion a nice plump shape.

Fold one end of wadding over the other, enclosing the smaller piece. Oversew roughly along the two side edges, leaving the bottom edge open.

Stuff the inside of the wadding with lavender, pot-pourri or another dried herb of your choice, and sew up the lower edge.

Fold the embroidered fabric over the wadding piece, and tack the folded edges together, enclosing it. Using stranded cotton (three strands), work blanket stitch around the edges, taking three threads with each stitch and spacing the stitches two fabric threads apart.

WORKING THE CORNER LOOPS At each corner of the pincushion, work three loops, as described on page 122. These are the traditional finishing touch for Assisi work items.

Use six strands of stranded cotton. Fasten the thread on the wrong side of the pincushion with a couple of tiny backstitches, then bring it through to the right side, three threads in from the edge. Take it to the back again through the same hole, forming a small loop, then bring it to the front, one thread up from the first entry.

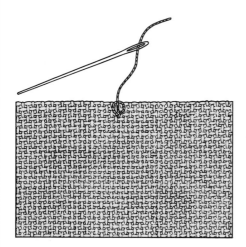

Making Assisi work loops: Step 1

Make a larger loop – about 2.5cm (1in) long (doubled) – and then take the needle to the back, through the same hole.

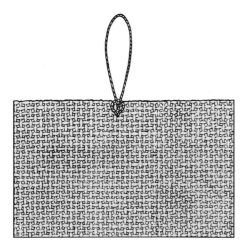

Step 2

Bring the needle to the front again, taking it over one or two fabric threads at the back so that the thread will not slip through, and form another long loop at the same point, again taking the needle to the back through the

same hole. Slip a finger through the two loops to make them the same size.

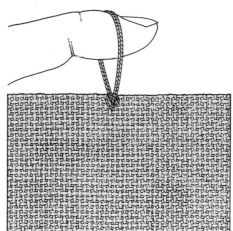

Step 3

Finally, bring the needle to the front again, inside the first loop, and take the thread around the two long loops and to the back.

Step 4

Draw up this last loop tightly, and fasten off neatly on the wrong side.

MAKING UP A CUSHION
The instructions that follow are the basic method of making up a cushion in which the front consists entirely of embroidery. For cushions with mitred fabric borders, see the additional instructions on page 123.

First cut a piece of fabric for the cushion back, the same size as the embroidery plus 2cm (¾in) all round.

Trim the front piece to the same size. Pin and tack [baste] the front and back together, with right sides facing, working from the front, just inside the seam allowance – that is, toward the centre.

Stitch the two pieces together, by machine or by hand, using backstitch, leaving a gap in the lower edge large enough for inserting the cushion – about 20–25cm (8–10in) is normally sufficient. Trim the seams to about 1cm (⅜in), and cut the corners diagonally to reduce the bulk.

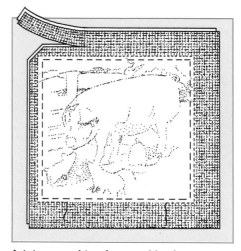

Joining a cushion front and back

Turn the cushion cover right side out, and insert the cushion pad. Close the gap with slipstitching, leaving a small hole near one corner. Push one end of the cord into this hole, then sew the cord over the seam, placing the stitches about 1cm (⅜in) apart.

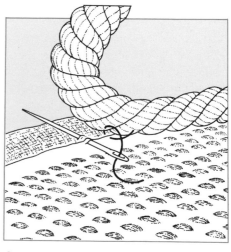

Sewing cord over a seam

At the corners you can make loops, as on the cushions in this book. Form the loop as shown and secure it on the underside of the cushion with a few stitches.

When you reach the starting point, trim the cord, leaving an end of about 2cm (¾in); slip this into the hole, crossing the first end at an angle, and close the gap with a few stitches, catching in the ends securely.

MITRED BORDER FOR A CUSHION When cutting pieces for a mitred border, remember – if you are using velvet or another napped or patterned fabric – to allow for the direction of the pile or pattern. Plan this on paper, and cut the border pieces accordingly.

Dimensions for the border strips are specified with the projects, but here is the method for establishing the size of borders for a cushion of a different size.

First decide on the overall size of the cushion, and cut a piece for the back to this size plus 2cm (¾in) all round. Subtract the *finished* size of the embroidery – that is, excluding seam allowance – from the finished overall size of the cushion. Thus, if the cushion will measure 40cm (16in) square, and the embroidery measures 30cm (12in) square, the difference is 10cm (4in). Divide this in half to get the finished width of each strip: 5cm (2in). Draw a paper pattern the length of the finished side by the finished width, then add 2cm (¾in) all round. Use this pattern to cut four border strips. (If the cushion is rectangular, you will, of course, have to cut two different lengths for the strips.)

Fold the corners of each strip to the wrong side, making a 45° angle; press. Mark the folds with tacking [basting] stitches, then cut off the corners, leaving a 2cm (¾in) seam allowance.

Stitch the four strips together, with right sides facing, along the line of tacking [basting]. Trim the seams and press them open. Turn under the seam allowance on the inner edge, unpicking a few stitches to allow the fabric to lie

Trimming a border strip

flat. Check the border against the embroidery to make sure it fits correctly. Press, then tack [baste] the seam allowance in place. Position the border around the embroidery, matching the edges exactly, and pin it in place. Slipstitch the border in place along the first unworked canvas thread outside the embroidery.

Join the cushion front and back as described on page 122.

Slipstitching the border

MAKING A TWISTED CORD
If you cannot find a suitable cord to edge a cushion, you can make your own, using the following method. Determine the number of strands required by twisting a few together tightly; add or subtract strands if necessary. Cut the required number of

strands for the cord, making them three times the finished length.

Tie the strands together at each end. Fasten one end to a drawer handle or another fixed point, and slip a pencil through the other knot. Pull the cord out straight from the drawer handle, then turn the pencil around clockwise until the strands are very tightly twisted. The cord should kink up in several places when you release the pressure.

Take both knots in one hand and give the cord a shake. It should coil around itself tightly. Smooth the coils if necessary, and tie a knot in each end. Trim both ends, cutting away the two original knots.

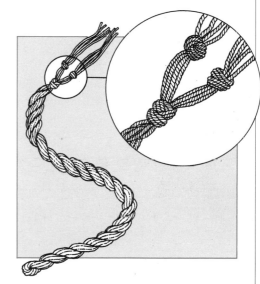

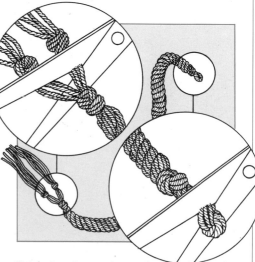

Trimming the two knotted ends of a cord

Place the piece of felt over the back and, using matching sewing thread and tiny stitches, oversew the front and back together. Leave a small hole at the bottom in which to push the ends of the braid. Push one end into the hole, then sew the braid around the edge, working on the front and using small oversewing stitches. When you reach the centre top of the design, form a loop with 11cm (4½in) of braid, sewing the braid together securely where it crosses. At the starting point, cut off the braid, leaving about 2cm (¾in) overlap. Push the end into the hole, and oversew to close it, arranging the braid so that it looks as if it continues unbroken around the edge. Oversew the braid to the back of the decoration.

CHRISTMAS TREE DECORATIONS

Lay the completed design, face up, on a piece of tracing paper and trace around it with a pencil. Remove the tracing paper, and cut around the pencil line. Place the tracing paper shape on the piece of felt, and draw round it with a pen. Cut out the shape, adding about 2mm ($\frac{1}{16}$in) all round.

Using the same paper template, cut out a piece of 2.5cm (1in)-thick wadding. Cut around the embroidered design, leaving a margin of 3cm (1¼in) all round. Place the embroidery face down on a flat surface, and place the piece of wadding on top. Fold the unworked edges of cloth back over the wadding, and stitch them together.

MAKING UP A PAPERWEIGHT

Trim the embroidered fabric so that it measures the same as the inside of the paperweight. Place the work face down into the upturned paperweight, then turn the paperweight right side up, to check that the design is correctly positioned. Turn it face down again, and position the card on the back. Remove the backing paper from the base fabric, and stick the fabric over the bottom of the paperweight.

MAKING UP A GREETINGS CARD

Place the card face down and open out both flaps. Lay the design face down over the hole. Mark the fabric just inside the two folds, so that it is slightly narrower than the centre panel, and trim all round to fit. Remove the embroidery and cover the inside of the card's centre panel with glue. Lay the design face up on the work surface and place the card face upwards over it. Spread glue around the inside edge of the left panel of the card and fold it down on to the back of the design.

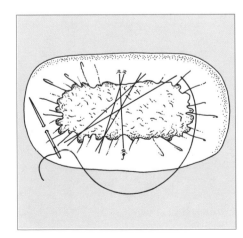

Lacing the fabric edges

Charting an Alphabet

This capital letter alphabet matches the lower-case alphabet used for the Seabird and Morning Glory samplers. If you prefer, you can use these alphabets for the birth sampler (page 86), rather than the ones used (shown complete on the Farmyard sampler, page 40).

To chart the lettering for a sampler, mark off on graph paper the exact number of squares to be included in the design. If you are using Aida cloth, this is simply the fabric count times the finished measurements in inches; if using single-thread evenweave or Hardanger, first divide the fabric count by the number of threads per stitch to get the stitches/spaces per inch.

When you have marked off the chart area, draw a line down the exact centre. The lettering should be centred around this line. You may wish to add the border motifs or other elements now.

Using extra graph paper (of the same scale), chart the alphabet, names and other lettering and numbers. Use ordinary pencil so that you can erase and adjust the spacing if necessary.

Cut out the strips containing the lettering, and move them around on the chart until you are pleased with the arrangement. Then tape them in place. The chart is now ready for use.

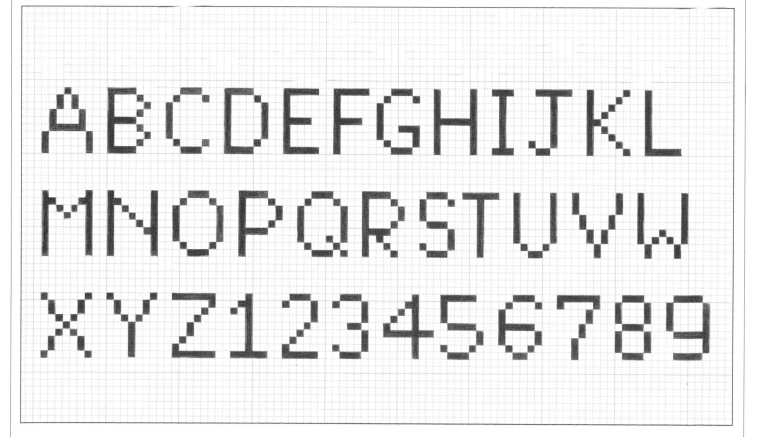

Kits and Suppliers

The designs listed below have been attractively packaged by *Needle Needs*. Each kit contains all the materials you require to complete the design. Only the finest quality materials are used.

The kits are available from local needlework shops (see list of stockists below), but, in case of difficulty, please send a self-addressed envelope to *Needle Needs*, Unit 21a, Silicon Centre, 26–28 Wadsworth Road, Perivale, Middlesex UB6 7JD for full details of how to purchase by mail order.

DISTRIBUTORS

UNITED KINGDOM AND EUROPE

NEEDLE NEEDS LTD,
Unit 21a, Silicon Centre, 26–28 Wadsworth Road, Perivale, Middlesex UB6 7JD.
Tel: (081) 991 9454 Fax: (081) 991 9506

AUSTRALIA

NEEDLE NEEDS, Lot 11, Mill Street, Mt Barker 6324, Western Australia.
Tel: (098) 512 030

STOCKISTS

The shops listed below carry materials used in stitching the projects contained in this book, together with the packaged kits produced by *Needle Needs*. With the exception of Craft Basics, they are also all agents for DMC. The materials and kits are also widely available through other good needlework outlets within the United Kingdom.

ARTISAN OF PINNER, 19–21 High Street, Pinner, Middlesex HA5 5PW

THE CAMPDEN NEEDLECRAFT CENTRE, High Street, Chipping Campden, Gloucestershire GL55 6AG

CRAFT BASICS, 2 Castlegate, Helmsley, North Yorkshire YO6 5AB

CREATIVITY, 45 New Oxford Street, London WC1A 1BH

THE GLASGOW NEEDLEWOMAN, 111 Candleriggs, Glasgow G1 1NP

LIBERTY, Regent Street, London W1R 6AH

MACE & NAIRN, 89 Crane Street, Salisbury, Wiltshire SP1 2PY

NEEDLESTYLE, 24–26 West Street, New Alresford, Near Winchester, Hampshire SO24 9AT

PISCES, 49 High Street, Ewell, Surrey KT17 1RX

REDBURN CRAFTS, Squire's Garden Centre, Halliford Road, Upper Halliford, Shepperton, Middlesex TW17 8RU

STITCHES, 355 Warwick Road, Solihull, West Midlands B91 1BQ

VOIRREY EMBROIDERY CENTRE, Brimstage Hall, Brimstage, Wirral, Merseyside L63 6JA

Information on other selected kits can be obtained from **GEMMA ATKINS,** 7 Penrose Terrace, Penzance, Cornwall TR18 2HQ

DMC PRODUCTS

Details of local DMC stockists can be obtained from: DMC **CREATIVE WORLD LTD,** Pullman Road, Wigston, Leicestershire LE18 2DY. Tel: (0533) 811040

EQUIPMENT SUPPLIERS

Pictures framed by:
PETE WAYNE, The Framing Studio, Bread Street, Penzance, Cornwall.
Tel: (0736) 60469

Antique velvet, braid and tassels bought from:
CATHERINE AND MARY ANTIQUES, 1 Brewery Yard, Bread Street, Penzance, Cornwall.
Tel: (0736) 51053

Pigs, geese, rabbits and sheep cushions made up by:
AFRA SINGER, The Workshop, Unit 4, Notley Farm, Long Crendon, Aylesbury, Bucks HP18 9ER. Tel: (0844) 208150

New braid bought from:
DISTINCTIVE TRIMMINGS, 17 Kensington Church Street, London W8 4LF. Tel: (071) 937 6174 (mail-order service available)

Some antiques and old postcards bought from:
BARBARA KIRK, Kitts Corner, 51 Chapel Street, Penzance, Cornwall. Tel: (0736) 64507

Other antiques from:
JANET DENISE, The Dorking Antique Centre, West Street, Dorking, Surrey.

Jetsetter desktop publishing program supplied by:
JETSETTER LTD, Bread Street, Penzance, Cornwall.
Tel: (0736) 67166

DMC STRANDED COTTON–TAPESTRY WOOL CONVERSION CHART

COTTON / WOOL	COTTON / WOOL	COTTON / WOOL	COTTON / WOOL	COTTON / WOOL	COTTON / WOOL	COTTON / WOOL	COTTON / WOOL
3713 / 7200	223 / 7194	3747 / 7799	807 / 7927	704 / 7548	832 / 7474	3770 / 7170	3032 / 7413
761 / 7132	3722 / 7195	341 / 7798	806 / 7960	703 / 7770	831 / 7573	951 / 7171	3781 / 7514
760 / 7760	3721 / 7691	340 / 7709	3765 / 7926	702 / 7345	830 / 7587	945 / 7164	3031 / 7489
3712 / 7759	221 / 7147	3746 / 7243	598 / 7399	701 / 7346	829 / 7490	3774 / 7121	422 / 7494
3328 / 7196	778 / 7211	333 / 7242	597 / 7927	700 / 7346	746 / écru	950 / 7192	420 / 7421
347 / 7127	3727 / 7251	327 / 7257	964 / 7958	699 / 7347	677 / 7579	3773 / 7950	869 / 7477
948 / 7170	316 / 7253	3753 / 7301	959 / 7545	989 / 7770	676 / 5543	3064 / 7166	977 / 7918
754 / 7471	3726 / 7226	3752 / 7828	958 / 7545	988 / 7769	729 / 7455	407 / 7165	976 / 7919
353 / 7170	315 / 7961	932 / 7594	943 / 7914	987 / 7768	680 / 7421	3772 / 7480	975 / 7700
352 / 7761	3354 / 7760	931 / 7593	928 / 7928	986 / 7387	3047 / 7501	632 / 7432	blanc neige/blanc
351 / 7356	3733 / 7759	930 / 7595	927 / 7323	524 / 7870	3046 / 7493	722 / 7918	3024 / 7282
350 / 7850	3731 / 7136	3750 / 7591	926 / 7927	523 / 7392	3045 / 7524	721 / 7922	3023 / 7509
349 / 7666	3350 / 7138	828 / 7599	3768 / 7690	522 / 7394	727 / 7727	720 / 7445	3022 / 7413
817 / 7666	3689 / 7211	827 / 7800	924 / 7926	520 / 7397	726 / 7726	402 / 7175	3787 / 7416
894 / 7605	3688 / 7151	813 / 7313	504 / 7400	772 / 7772	725 / 7725	3776 / 7766	3021 / 7533
893 / 7135	3687 / 7602	826 / 7996	503 / 7704	3364 / 7424	783 / 7782	301 / 7457	822 / écru
892 / 7136	3685 / 7212	825 / 7995	502 / 7335	3363 / 7427	782 / 7705	400 / 7401	644 / 7271
891 / 7640	605 / 7133	824 / 7650	501 / 7702	3362 / 7396	781 / 7833	300 / 7459	642 / 7509
819 / 7200	604 / 7605	3756 / 7587	500 / 7429	907 / 7584	780 / 7508	712 / 7491	640 / 7355
818 / 7132	603 / 7153	775 / 7301	993 / 7952	906 / 7547	745 / 7579	739 / 7461	3790 / 7391
776 / 7202	602 / 7603	3325 / 7302	992 / 7598	905 / 7988	744 / 7503	738 / 7143	372 / 7523
3326 / 7133	601 / 7600	3755 / 7313	991 / 7906	904 / 7768	743 / 7725	437 / 7455	371 / 7254
899 / 7204	600 / 7600	334 / 7283	564 / 7958	472 / 7470	742 / 7742	436 / 7455	370 / 7525
335 / 7205	3743 / 7722	322 / 7316	563 / 7545	471 / 7459	741 / 7741	435 / 7846	613 / 7511
309 / 7640	3042 / 7241	312 / 7311	562 / 7909	470 / 7583	740 / 7740	434 / 7508	612 / 7413
326 / 7640	3041 / 7262	311 / 7336	561 / 7541	469 / 7364	608 / 7946	433 / 7845	611 / 7415
957 / 7605	3740 / 7266	336 / 7307	966 / 7382	937 / 7393	606 / 7606	001 / 7479	010 / 7410
956 / 7135	3609 / 7896	823 / 7299	955 / 7954	936 / 7425	3078 / 7905	898 / 7801	453 / 7300
963 / 7132	3608 / 7251	939 / 7299	954 / 7542	935 / 7379	445 / 7431	938 / 7467	452 / 7280
3716 / 7133	3607 / 7255	800 / 7799	913 / 7604	934 / 7359	307 / 7433	3371 / 7533	451 / 7273
962 / 7204	718 / 7153	809 / 7798	912 / 7912	3053 / 7424	444 / 7435	3379 / 7192	535 / 7622
961 / 7205	917 / 7255	799 / 7314	911 / 7911	3052 / 7362	973 / 7973	758 / 7164	3072 / 7715
3708 / 7103	915 / 7210	798 / 7317	910 / 7943	3051 / 7377	972 / 7971	3778 / 7124	648 / 7617
3706 / 7104	554 / 7709	797 / 7318	909 / 7915	3013 / 7363	971 / 7437	356 / 7146	647 / 7282
3705 / 7106	553 / 7895	796 / 7797	369 / 7420	3012 / 7425	970 / 7947	355 / 7184	646 / 7273
666 / 7666	552 / 7708	820 / 7820	368 / 7369	3011 / 7355	947 / 7947	3777 / 7447	645 / 7275
321 / 7107	550 / 7245	747 / 7828	320 / 7384	581 / 7583	946 / 7439	écru / écru	844 / 7622
304 / 7108	211 / 7709	3761 / 7828	367 / 7320	580 / 7393	900 / 7360	543 / 7460	762 / 7715
498 / 7110	210 / 7709	519 / 7298	319 / 7387	734 / 7423	3341 / 7123	842 / 7230	415 / 7715
816 / 7138	209 / 7711	518 / 7813	890 / 7398	733 / 7363	3340 / 7124	841 / 7232	318 / 7758
815 / 7139	208 / 7708	3760 / 7996	3348 / 7382	732 / 7573	922 / 7922	840 / 7518	414 / 7618
814 / 7219	794 / 7302	517 / 7995	3347 / 7384	731 / 7582	921 / 7176	839 / 7432	317 / 7622
902 / 7115	793 / 7314	996 / 7996	3346 / 7376	730 / 7355	920 / 7446	838 / 7938	413 / 7713
225 / 7200	792 / 7797	995 / 7995	3345 / 7427	834 / 7503	919 / 7178	3033 / 7450	3799 / 7694
224 / 7193	791 / 7796	3766 / 7399	895 / 7396	833 / 7473	918 / 7447	3782 / 7520	310 / noir

Acknowledgements

I should like to thank my husband, Gareth, for his help in stretching the canvases and sorting out the computer when I got into a mess with it – and also for writing a computer symbol program for the charts, even though it was not used. I should like to thank him, my children, Lucy, Gemma, Rose, Ellie, Alice and Jack, and my grandchildren, Rhiannon, Bethany and Joshua, for putting up without complaint with my working seven days a week for eleven months on this book; Gemma for her help with the typing; and Lucy, Ellie and Alice for their help with colouring the charts.

I should also like to thank Lyn Le Grice for writing the foreword and for her faith in me and her help and encouragement over the years; Francine Lawrence for her help, and for giving me my first big break in *Country Living* magazine; Eunice Chapman and Tessa Hilton for giving me my first magazine design work in *Mother* magazine; Carol James of *Baby* magazine, who got me started on embroidery; Chris Kirk and Julie Harris for their enthusiasm and encouragement; Cara Ackerman of DMC Creative World Ltd for all her help, and for the introduction to Collins & Brown; Gabrielle Townsend for contracting me to write this book; Eleanor Van Zandt for her help in editing the book; Jetsetter Ltd, for supplying their desktop publishing program for me to use and for their invaluable hot-line support; Stitches of Penzance for supplying DMC products; and Paula Bell, Joan Riseam, Colleen Selby and Brenda Vowles for their help in making up the designs.

Finally, thanks to my mother and father, Lydia and Arthur Ellis, and to my aunts and uncles, Lydia and John Davies, Hilda Thomas, and Edna and Phillips Richards, for the wonderful holidays on the north and south coasts of Wales when I was a child, which inspired this book.